MEDITATIONS AND CEREMONIES FOR HEALING

A Handbook for Personal Growth and Wellness

MONIQUE LANG

BALBOA.
PRESS

A DIVISION OF HAY HOUSE

Copyright © 2019 Monique Lang.

All rights reserved. No part of this book may be used or reproduced by any means, graphic, electronic, or mechanical, including photocopying, recording, taping or by any information storage retrieval system without the written permission of the author except in the case of brief quotations embodied in critical articles and reviews.

The information, ideas, and suggestions in this book are not intended as a substitute for professional advice. Before following any suggestions contained in this book, you should consult your personal physician or mental health professional. Neither the author nor the publisher shall be liable or responsible for any loss or damage allegedly arising as a consequence of your use or application of any information or suggestions in this book.

This book is a work of non-fiction. Unless otherwise noted, the author and the publisher make no explicit guarantees as to the accuracy of the information contained in this book and in some cases, names of people and places have been altered to protect their privacy.

Balboa Press books may be ordered through booksellers or by contacting:

Balboa Press
A Division of Hay House
1663 Liberty Drive
Bloomington, IN 47403
www.balboapress.com
1 (877) 407-4847

Because of the dynamic nature of the Internet, any web addresses or links contained in this book may have changed since publication and may no longer be valid. The views expressed in this work are solely those of the author and do not necessarily reflect the views of the publisher, and the publisher hereby disclaims any responsibility for them.

The author of this book does not dispense medical advice or prescribe the use of any technique as a form of treatment for physical, emotional, or medical problems without the advice of a physician, either directly or indirectly. The intent of the author is only to offer information of a general nature to help you in your quest for emotional and spiritual well-being. In the event you use any of the information in this book for yourself, which is your constitutional right, the author and the publisher assume no responsibility for your actions.

Any people depicted in stock imagery provided by Getty Images are models, and such images are being used for illustrative purposes only.
Certain stock imagery © Getty Images.

Print information available on the last page.

ISBN: 978-1-9822-1653-5 (sc)
ISBN: 978-1-9822-1652-8 (hc)
ISBN: 978-1-9822-1658-0 (e)

Library of Congress Control Number: 2018913817

Balboa Press rev. date: 12/12/2018

MEDITATIONS

INTRODUCTION

For years now I have started many individual psychotherapy sessions, supervision groups, workshops, and meetings with a short meditation to set a tone for the experience.

I use some of these meditations to create a safe, easy, non-judging space in which people can do the work of healing and of sharing difficult material. I think of these meditations as an invitation—an invitation into presence, caring and compassion.

Other meditations are geared to connecting with your own inner knowing, your memories, your sensations, and, at times, with issues that have been buried deep inside your psyche.

Over the years many of my students and clients have asked me what sources I use to find the meditations that I offer. The truth is that they come up spontaneously in response to what is happening in the room energetically at the moment, or what space I want to create, or what material I want to either elicit or heal.

Although there are many styles of meditation from a variety of traditions, the meditations in this book are geared to self-knowing, healing, and relaxation.

The meditations offered here are very simple and basic. I offer them as an invitation—an invitation for you to use them as a primer, a stepping stone. My hope is that you will create your own by changing and designing them to meet the intent for which you will be using them.

If you already have a meditation practice, you can easily integrate some of the ideas in this book with the style that you currently practice.

At the end of each meditation, there is an empty "notes" section. This is provided for you to jot down anything that has meaning for you, or any thoughts or insights you want to remember.

At the beginning and end of some of the meditations, there are notes for those of you who are clinicians. Even if you are not, you are welcome to use the suggestions given there if they feel helpful to you. Or, if you are working with a clinician, you can bring whatever came up for you to work on with that person.

The meditations are arranged in a loose sequence, however you are invited and encouraged to choose those that call to you at a particular time, regardless of order.

In beauty always, ✽
Monique

In Beauty May I walk—A Navajo Blessing

With beauty before me I walk
With beauty behind me I walk
With beauty above me I walk
With beauty around me I walk

Today I will walk out, today everything unnecessary will leave me, I will be as I was before, I will have a cool breeze over my body. I will have a light body, I will be happy forever; nothing will hinder me.

NOTE FOR CLINICIANS

This chapter is meant as a basic template for clinicians who wish to use some of these meditations in their practice.

To start with, I must explain that although I have certifications in many modalities of psychotherapy which show up in the vocabulary that I use throughout, my main framework is based on Internal Family Systems (Dr. Richard Schwartz), which posits that we all have a "Self," which some people refer to as our essence. We also have many "parts" (some healthy, others burdened) that have a variety of functions to help us navigate life. Hence much of the language, and concepts, that I use throughout this manuscript reflect that way of interpreting one's psyche.

When doing a meditation—or mindfulness exercise—with someone for the first time, I will preface the exercise by asking the client if s/he/they is willing to try an experiment. I also reassure her that we can stop at any time if the process feels uncomfortable, or in any way negative.

I avoid words like "dis-regulating" or "triggering" or any word that I know might be difficult for my client to hear. I endeavor to maintain as much neutral, everyday language as possible. This way it doesn't sound to "woo woo" (as one of my students referred to it). Always ask permission. If the person you are working with doesn't want to do the exercise, you can explore the reasons, and investigate what parts have concerns, but do not do a meditation until you have agreement from all parts. Doing a mindfulness exercise without expressed consent is a recipe for failure.

Many clients want to know—to understand—why you want them to do this meditation or why they should imagine situations. This is my typical answer, though I encourage you to craft your own:

I would like to introduce these meditations/relaxation/mindfulness practices because many scientific studies now show that calming the mind and the body is an effective way to relieve stress, fear, nervousness, sleeplessness, worry, anxiety and even pain (Jon Kabat-Zin)—both physical and emotional. Mindfulness practice also opens up some emotional room to work with difficult material without becoming flooded or overwhelmed.

Mindfulness techniques have been shown to help us gain greater clarity of thought and feeling. These practices enable us to connect with aspects of ourselves (parts) that have been buried in our unconscious and often carry negative beliefs and decisions about who we are and how we need to lead our lives. Lastly, it has been my experience that working in this way allows for the client's system to feel safe enough and grounded enough to work with traumatic material.

I recommend that you begin with short sets—maybe 3 minutes maximum. For someone who is new at this practice, it can feel like a really long time.

As you and your client become more comfortable with the practice you can extend the time to almost the whole session, with the client being 'inside' in a meditative process.

It is vital that you let your client know that there is no "right" or "wrong" way to do this, and that the information that they receive is perfect for the moment. Even if they "can't do it," it is grist for the mill. It is also helpful to remind your clients that, like most things, these practices become easier over time as the system becomes entrained. Over time, you and your client will feel safer and more comfortable with this way of working. I often remind my clients that when they first learned to walk or roller skate, they fell many, many times!

When you are saying a meditation, make sure you speak:

- Very slowly - You will learn to adjust you tempo in partnership with your client.
- Softly - drop your pitch and your tone. That prosody will help create safety.
- Allow for time between sentences - One breath between sentences is a good beginning. 15-30 seconds can be a good tempo, though it might feel like a long time at first. After a while, you can easily go over a minute depending on what you are asking your client to do and/or if your client is comfortable in the silence.

Personal Notes—Use this space to make your own annotations or observations.

Basic Setting

When preparing for a meditation—or mindfulness exercise—it is preferable to have the right setting. It should be one that will prevent distractions. Let go of all of your electronics and find a quiet and safe space where you will not be disturbed. It can be anywhere, including the bathroom if need be. It can be a corner of a room that you will return to over and over to do this practice, it can be a favorite chair or couch, a cushion on the floor, etc. You can designate that area with a special object, such as a stone, a flower, or a picture. Anything that is meaningful to you.

It is helpful to use the same space over and over. This allows for what is called *entrainment*—to fall into synchronicity with. It's a little bit like the Pavlovian concept of a conditioned reflex. Over time it supports and enhances the meditation practices because it lets your system know that when you go to this place, that is what you will do.

Unless you are already a meditator, I suggest that you start with three to five minutes. This can feel like a long time! Through regular practice you can extend the time as you become more comfortable and skilled.

The order of the meditations in this book is meant to support this. The earlier meditations are shorter, and as you move through the book, they become lengthier.

Remember—there is no right or wrong way to do this. Meditation, like many other things, is a skill that develops over time. One of my teachers used to say to me, "You don't have to do it right, and you can't do it wrong." (Not that I'm a perfectionist!)

It might be helpful for you to record the meditation that you want to do or have someone lead you through it rather than have to read each line or try to remember the whole thing.

Induction

There is a reminder at the beginning of each meditation to use the induction.

You can use this one, or you can make up your own. It does help to be consistent, since it helps both brain and body to be ready for what is to come. Even if you know this induction well (or any other that you prefer), it helps to say it out loud if you are voicing the meditation for someone else; this will establish a connection between you and the other person, and it also help create an inner connection for the person who will be doing the meditation.

If you are doing the meditation on your own, you might want to say it to yourself either out loud or in your head.

This is the standard induction I use. Each end of a sentence represents a short pause—a breath.

❊ ❊ ❊

Begin by placing both feet on the ground.
If you feel comfortable, close your eyes. If not, allow yourself to have "soft eyes"—focusing gently on something innocuous, like a spot on the ground or on the wall, the leg of a chair, etc., about a foot ahead of you.

Uncross your legs.
Uncross your arms.

Begin by noticing your breath.
Breathing in ...
Breathing out ...

Breathe in through your nose.
Breathe out through your mouth.

Allow your breath to become slower and deeper.
Continue this breathing for a couple of minutes.

If this is your first time, this can be a good place to stop and check in on the experience of simply breathing, or you can move on to one of the guided meditations that follows.

NOTES

Beginning Awareness Practice

Induction

Slowly ...

Notice your feet on the ground—
    Notice how they feel in your shoes or on the floor or cushion.
    Where do they touch?
    Does it feel good or hard or tight or ...?
You can adjust or simply notice the feeling.

Notice your buttocks on the chair or couch or floor—
    Where do they touch?
    How does it feel? Is it soft or hard?
You can adjust or simply notice the feeling.

Allow your spine to lengthen and relax,
    As if there were a ray of light or bubble of space between each vertebrae.
    Imagine that your head is floating gently on top of your spine.

Return your attention to your breath ...
    Breathing in... Breathing out. ...

Become aware of the sounds around you.
Notice the energy in your surroundings.
Notice the light.

Notice any changes within you—
- In your thoughts ...
- In your physical being ...
- In your emotions.

NOTES

Thoughts, Feelings, and Sensations

Induction

While practicing a meditation or relaxation technique, thoughts, feelings, sensations, and memories are bound to crop up; they will undoubtedly begin to engage all of your attention, causing you to forget that you were breathing or scanning your body. This is normal. The mind likes to be engaged. The challenge is to help the mind return to the endeavor at hand, with gentleness.

At times the thoughts, feelings, and sensations that arise are lovely and soothing. It may be worthwhile letting yourself bask in the comfort of these images, thoughts, or feelings rather than struggle to go back to the original intention. On the other hand, this might be a diversion that prevents you from doing the work that you wanted to do. In that case, gently return to your original intention, letting yourself know that you can come back to these feelings, thoughts, memories, or sensations at any time.

If you find yourself getting distracted by your shopping list, your to-do list, the sound of the cars going by, or your thoughts about someone you care about, it is helpful to acknowledge the distraction, name it, and return to your breath. Telling these distractions to go away or trying to ignore them typically doesn't work, although that is what most of us try to do. It is paradoxical but true that the more you try to make them go away, the more they stick.

Conversely, if you can acknowledge and accept those thoughts, feelings, or memories without trying to change them, they will loosen their grip on your mind. Obviously this is easier said than done, but with time and practice, as we soften around those distractions, it becomes easier to do.

A wonderful mantra that I learned from Tara Brach is to bring acceptance to whatever comes up with the phrase "and this too." This way you acknowledge what is going on and put it in the larger context of many thoughts, feelings, sensations, or memories.

Another way to focus is to notice something positive and neutral: the warmth in your hands, the sun outside, the support of your chair, your breath, etc.

On the other hand, particularly at times of stress, pain, or strife, your feelings, sensations, and memories can be unpleasant or scary and can lead you into a downward spiral into worse and worse scenarios.

At those times, it might be wise to come out of the meditation—particularly if you are alone. On the other hand, if you are with someone you trust and who can hold space for you, you can engage with those thoughts, feelings, or memories to heal them.

Following are some techniques that can be helpful. And remember that with practice it becomes easier—remember how hard it was when you baked your first cake or learned to ride a bike?

1. When a thought, a feeling, a sensation, or a memory comes into your awareness, name it. For example, if you are feeling scared, annoyed, sad, worried, or restless, say to yourself, "I'm feeling …" without trying to make the feeling go away or change it and without judging it—with compassion. It is quite a feat to just be with whatever is coming up, and that in of itself will change it.
2. Another technique is to acknowledge the thought, feeling, or sensation, and then imagine it passing through your consciousness as if it were a cloud moving across

the sky or a stick floating down a river. So, it is there, and it passes.
3. Use your breath. Consciously breathe in the thought, feeling, or sensation and then, on the exhale, imagine that thought, feeling, or sensation moving out of your body. You might give it a shape, a color, or an image to help move it out.
4. If the thoughts, feelings, or sensations that you are experiencing are overwhelming you, change your focus. Move your body, look at something pleasant, listen to some music, go for a walk, or call a friend.

NOTES

Thinking Mind

It is the nature of the mind to think. However, quite often our thoughts go on and on without allowing us a moment of rest.

This meditation offers you a way to calm the mind and to let go of thoughts, particularly those repetitive thoughts that actually don't serve us and just keep us worried and anxious.

❉ ❉ ❉

Induction

As you sit quietly, become aware of the thoughts coursing through your mind.

Ask the part of you that thinks constantly whether it would be willing to show itself.
How old is it?
How did it get created?
How does it serve you?
Did it come about to protect you in some way?
What does that part believe would happen if it did not keep you so occupied?
How do you feel towards it?

Take a couple of minutes to be with that part and hear it out.
Now ask that part whether it would be willing to step back and allow you to just *be*.
Notice any other parts that have concerns about not thinking.

Ask them to step back for a little while as well, reassuring them that you will return your attention to them when you are finished with the present meditation.

Observe what happens if those parts actually move aside for a bit.

Take a minute or so to perceive what it's like to not be thinking.

Thank your thinking parts for their willingness to show up and to give you a little space.

Ask them whether they would be amenable to giving you some leeway in your everyday life, and/or whether they would acquiesce to letting you do this practice again.

NOTES

Working with the Breath

Induction

Become aware of your breath without trying to change it in any way.
Just notice its rhythm.
Keep your awareness on your breath.
Breathing in through your nostrils, breathing out through your mouth.
Now, gently, allow your breath to deepen.
Feel your breath coming into your lung, filling your lungs, moving down all the way into your belly, filling it up like a balloon.
You might want to add words like:

* Breathing in, I breathe in peace, love, compassion, gentleness, calm.
* Breathing out, I let go of hurt, pain, sadness, anger, fear.

Or you may repeat a "mantra" which is a word repeated over and over.
For example you can say "love" on the in breath and you can repeat "love" on the out breath.
Don't worry about intruding distractions, just let them float through your mind as clouds in the sky (If this is a challenge, go back to "working with thoughts, feelings, and sensations.")
3 -10 minutes is a good time frame to begin with.
If you want to deepen the practice, imagine breathing in from the bottom of your spine and allowing the breath to move up into your head and then exhaling down the front of your

body and returning to the bottom of your spine, moving up your spine and down the front of your body in one continuous circle.

When you feel done, gently return your breath to its normal rhythm.

Notice your surroundings and let yourself return to this time and place.

NOTES

Body Scan

This short meditation is a good way to begin focusing on the sensations in our bodies.

※ ※ ※

This meditation should be done slowly.
Try to take at least one breath before moving on to the next part of your body.

Notice your feet on the ground…
Notice your buttocks on the chair, couch or ground …
Allow your spine to lengthen and relax …
Imagine that your head is floating easily on the top of your spine.
Focus your attention on your breath for a minute or so.
Breathing in… breathing out.
Notice the sensation of your feet on the ground.
If you are wearing shoes, notice how your feet feel in them…
Are they spacious, tight, comforting, itchy …?
You don't have to change anything. Just notice.

Notice the sensation of your buttocks on the couch, chair or ground.
    Where do they make contact…?
    Is that contact soft or hard…?
    Is it comfortable or not…?
    What is it like to actually feel your buttocks touching a surface…?
    Can you feel your thighs?

What other parts of your body are you aware of?

Where are your hands resting…?
How does it feel to touch that part of your body…?
How do your hands feel…?
Are they warm or cold…?
Are they relaxed or tight…?
Straight or curled?

What else are you noticing?
What is it like to be in such intimate connection with your body? Take as long as you want to continue this exploration and when you are done, return your attention to your breath and let yourself come back to this place and time.

NOTES

Total Body Relaxation

This is a great meditation for relaxation. It is similar to yoga nidra (yogic sleep). In this exercise, you do not move your body, you simply send out the mental directive to the part of your body that you are relaxing. Some other models ask you to tense and release certain muscles. This one does not.

This meditation is also terrific if you are having trouble sleeping. It can help you fall asleep or if you are one of those people who wake up in the middle of the night and can't go back to sleep, this might help you fall back asleep, and if not, it will help distract your mind and focus on something other than the worries that are presently occupying it.

If you are doing this meditation as a relaxation, you might want to set an alarm so you don't have to worry if you do fall asleep. If you are ready to go to sleep, let yourself.

You might want to have someone read you this meditation or record it and play it to yourself. (I also have an audio that you can access through my website—moniquelanglcsw.com)

Again, this a mental exercise; there is no need to move. It is actually recommended that you not. Merely focus on the different parts of your body and send the instruction to relax. Also, particularly if you are planning to go to sleep, it's a great idea to lie down.

❋ ❋ ❋

Induction

Take a couple of deep breaths.
Begin with your feet and slowly move your focus up your body.

You might want to take at least one inhale/exhale between each part that you relax.

Be aware that some parts of your body may have difficulties relaxing. Do not fight it, just notice it and move on to the next area.

Relax you toes ...
Relax your ankles ...
Relax your shins - and relax your calves...
Relax your knees - the top of your knees and the back of your knees...
Relax your thighs - the front of your thighs - and relax your hamstrings ...
Relax your hips and your hipbones ...
Relax your pelvis and relax your pelvic bowl...
Relax your belly and all the organs in your belly...
Relax your solar plexus...
Relax your chest ...
Relax your lungs and relax your heart area ...
Relax your collarbones ...
Relax your arms ...
Relax your hands and your fingers ...
Relax your neck ...
Relax your throat ...
Relax your jaw ...
Relax your face ...
Relax your eyes and your eyebrows ...
Relax your forehead ...
Relax your head—
    the right side of your head, the left side of your head, the back of your head ...
Relax your brain ...!
Relax the back of your neck...
Relax your shoulder blades ...

Relax your upper back ...
Relax your middle back ...
Relax your lower back—relax your tailbone.

Take a couple of deep breaths. This is a good place to let yourself float back to consciousness.

If you have the time, and are curious, you can notice the parts that relaxed easily. You can also connect with parts that may have not been able to relax and be curious about the tension that they hold. Gently and compassionately ask those parts what prevents them from relaxing. What are they holding? What would they need to relax? Could it be rest, or compassion, or love, or understanding, or exercise or ...? If possible, give that part whatever it needs either in your mind's eye or in the external reality.

NOTES

Enhancing Positive Body Sensations

The purpose of this meditation is to focus on and enhance physical body sensations that feel pleasurable. We often focus on those parts of our body that are in pain or are not working to our satisfaction. This is a wonderful exercise to begin practicing positivity in our physical being. The more we learn to do that, the more our body/mind will respond to focusing on wellbeing.

As strange as it might sound, this is a great exercise for those of us who suffer from physical pain because the pain usually takes up most of our attention. This exercise helps change the focus to areas of our body that are pain free, even if it is the tip of one finger to start off with.

❊ ❊ ❊

Induction

Begin by scanning your physical body.
You can either start at your head and move downward, or begin at your feet and move upward.
Become aware of **any** positive sensation.

It could be warmth, a sense of ease, or a feeling of relaxation.
It might be very small and quite subtle,
Or it might be quite noticeable.

Once you have found the pleasant sensation, you might want to give it a color, or an image, or a shape.
Take your time to focus on the pleasant sensation and to bathe in it.

Now see if you can expand this positive sensation so that it radiates throughout your entire body. Best not to hold judgement as to where it goes, or doesn't go. Trust your body's wisdom.

Take your time.

Place your right hand on any part of your body that feels right, and give yourself the following instruction: I can remember/recapture this feeling of well being by placing my hand on that part of my body and re-membering.

Take a couple of deep breaths and let yourself come back to this time and place.

NOTES

Working with Pain or Discomfort

Many of us are challenged by pain—physical pain and emotional pain. If it is emotional pain, it is helpful for this meditation if you can locate where in your body you feel it. Do you feel anger or fear in your solar plexus, sadness in your chest, anxiety in your head or your belly. This is actually a good first step to working with emotional pain.

❄ ❄ ❄

Induction

Very gently bring your focus to the part of your body that holds discomfort. It might be actual physical pain—a sprained ankle—or an emotional pain that you feel in your body.

Notice where in your body you feel the discomfort or pain.
Does it have a color…?
or a shape…?
What is the sensation…?
is it hot or cold, or tight or heavy…?
Does it have a sound…?
Does it have a taste…?
Does it have a smell…?

Ask how long this pain/discomfort has been with you?
What caused it?
Was it sudden or did it get created over time?
Is it physically based, emotionally based, or both?

What would happen if it wasn't there...?
Would that be okay...?
What would happen in your life if it wasn't there?

What does the part that holds the pain need...?
Can you give that part what it needs in your mind's eyes?
Can you make changes in your life to help that part feel better?

Sometimes those parts just need to be noticed and sent compassion and understanding.
(If it needs something from the outside, is that a reasonable request? Are you likely to get it?)

Now that you have given the part that holds pain your attention, how does it feel now?
Does it need anything else?
Can you make a commitment to check in with that part over the next while to see how it's doing?

When you are ready, bring your attention back to your breath.
Breathing in ...Breathing out.

Feel your feet on the ground, your buttocks on the chair.
And when you are ready let yourself come back to this time and place.

NOTES

Releasing Painful Energy

Induction

Gently focus your attention on any part of your physical, mental, or emotional bodies that hold pain.

>Give this part a shape, or a color, or an image.

>Softly imagine that painful energy coming out of every cell of your physical, mental or emotional bodies.

You can send it:
to the earth to be composted,
to the water to be carried away,
to the wind to be blown away,
to the fire to be burned off,
or wherever seems like a good place to send it for recycling.

You do not want to send it to any being to hurt them.

Take a couple of minutes to do this.

Give thanks to whatever element you chose for transmuting this negative energy.

>When you feel as cleared as you can get for now (you can always repeat the process), imagine this gentle, soft, loving, powerful, healing energy coming into every pore of your physical, emotional and mental bodies replacing that which has been discarded.

Take a couple of minutes to let in the good energy (notice if it's hard for you ... do it anyway!)

When you are ready, return your attention to your breath. Breathing in... Breathing out.

And let yourself come back to this time and place.

NOTES

Releasing Negativity

Many of us continue to hold on to negative ways of thinking and live with a glass half empty attitude, or one that views most events from a gloomy perspective. I'm not suggesting that you become blinded to the many horrible things happening in our world. However, changing your mind set will change your life for the better (I know, my mother's idea of a positive was a double negative!) And changing your attitude also helps everyone around you.

❋ ❋ ❋

Induction

Becoming aware of your thinking, notice where your mind goes.
Notice the patterns of negativity.
Give the part that holds those patterns a color, a shape, or an image.

How did that part/that attitude come to be?
Does it belong to you …
or is it a pattern that you picked up from your lineage or your culture?
Does that way of thinking come from situations you've been in?

What if you transform it?
What if you could live from a more positive mindset?
What would that be like?

Imagine this part that holds negative patterns of seeing the world coming out of your brain as the color, the shape, or the image that you gave it.

Or you can envision this negative pattern as an energy moving out of your head and out to the universe to be transformed into pure light.

Now softly imagine what positive thinking would look like…?
What would it feel like…?
Give that positivity a color, or a shape, or an image.
Imagine that positive energy coming into your head, filling up all the places that were occupied by negative thinking.

When you are ready,
take a couple of deep breaths.
Breathing in… Breathing out.

And let yourself come back to this time and place.

NOTES

Bringing in Healing Energy

This is an excellent segue to the previous meditation in which you worked on letting go of negative energy.

This should be done **very** slowly. If you are talking someone through it, make sure you pause often. If you are doing it for yourself and are recording it, give yourself lots of time between each invitation.

❈ ❈ ❈

Induction

Imagine a beautiful, shimmering, healing light or energy hovering over your head.
You might want to give it a color or colors.
(There isn't a color that is better than another. What you get is perfect.)

Envision this energy, this shimmering healing, loving, light coming in through the top of your head…
bathing your entire head and brain…
relaxing your thoughts …
healing any negative ideas.

Allow this shimmering, healing, energy to move down into your face…
soothing any tension or stress that is held there.

Let this healing, loving, light move into your neck and your shoulders …

releasing any tension that is held there.

Continue to let this loving, healing, energy move into your chest…
into your lungs …
surrounding your heart,…
healing and soothing any wounds or sorrows.

Visualize this healing light moving into your solar plexus …
down into your belly…
relaxing… healing…nurturing.

Enable this light to flow into your pelvic bowl,
and into your hips …
moving down your legs, and into your feet…
and flowing out of the soles of your feet into the earth,
connecting and anchoring you into solid ground.

Pause at least 30 seconds

Feel the solid, healing, energy of the earth coming into your body through the soles of your feet …moving up your legs, filling… fortifying your body.

Imagine this beautiful, grounding, energy moving up into your pelvic bowl, replenishing you.

Allow this earth connecting energy to continue moving up into your solar plexus, bringing power, and courage and healing.

Let this substantial, grounding energy move up into your chest and your lungs,
bringing stability and strength.

Visualize this strong, beautiful, grounding energy moving into your neck, stabilizing and energizing.

Bring this earth grounding energy into your face…
into your head and your brain … bringing grounding and strength.

Continuing to move this strong grounding energy up, past the crown of your head,
connecting with the shimmering light energy of above.

Allow yourself to feel healed, grounded and energized by the shimmering light energy from above intertwined with the grounded, solid, energy of below.

Take a couple of minutes to feel yourself complete.

Breathe in… Breathe out.

And when you are ready let yourself come back to this time and place.

NOTES

Healing the Heart

Who has not suffered from a wounded heart?

This mediation is similar to the previous meditation, Bringing in Healing Energy, however, this meditation focuses on the heart.

Induction

Focus your attention to your heart area and imagine a lovely, shimmering, healing light or energy coming into your heart area.

Allow this light or energy to fill your chest.

As you experience this shimmering, loving, compassionate, light or energy, you might want to give it a color, or a shape, or an image.

Allow this light to surround your heart, bringing in gentleness and kindness into your heart.

Now, very gently, allow memories of hurts, or of pains, or of sorrows to come out of your heart and into this energy of love, gentleness, and kindness.
Take your time…
If tears come, let them flow to cleanse the hurt out.
Let each situation, each wound, come out and let it be released from your heart.

Give each hurt/wounded part of yourself the time to feel witnessed, held and comforted by this loving healing energy.

Continue for a little while to let this beautiful, healing, loving, energy sooth the pain and sorrow that those parts have carried.

Keep breathing into this energy of healing.

When you feel ready, place your left hand on your heart, and let yourself know that you can reconnect to this energy of healing any time just by putting your hand on your heart and re-membering.

When you are ready ...
return your attention to your breath.
Breathing in... Breathing out.

Feel your feet on the ground ...
and slowly open your eyes and be here.

NOTES

Gratitude

According to many spiritual teachers, gratitude is an attitude. It is a life's view.

This is a very short, simple meditation that was gifted to me by one of my teachers when I felt that everything in my life was falling apart and I was rather miserable. It is lovely even when all is going well for you.

❊ ❊ ❊

Induction

In your mind's eye review the day and note/acknowledge all the things that you are grateful for that happened that day.

It is recommended that you come up with at least 10 things. Of course you can do more. You can be grateful for really simple things like you had hot water, or the sun was shining, or you have a job, etc.

You can then expand the practice to whatever you are grateful for in your life in general.

If you are feeling brave, review the difficult times or situations in your life and detect the lessons in those situations that you can be grateful for. Sometimes a negative event can be seen from a place of gratitude, if we can acknowledge what we learned as a consequence of that event and how we have grown as a result of having gone through the experience.

NOTES

A Place of Rest

Some times in the hustle and bustle of our lives, it is difficult to find a moment to shut out all the outside noises and demands, or to have a place of one's own to be quiet or reflective. This meditation will help you to create that space for yourself.

※ ※ ※

Note to clinicians. This meditation is also very helpful as a resource for people who were abused and felt that they had no place to be safe. You can help them create a place where they can bring their young, wounded/scared, parts so that their adults can function in the world with greater freedom and ease.

※ ※ ※

Induction

In your mind's eye allow yourself to imagine a wondrous place.
It might be inside or outside...
It might be a place you know well,
or a place you are creating as you go.

Feel free to make it exactly the way you would like it, a place where you would feel safe and comfortable. There are no rules. You can have a fireplace on the beach, trees in a bedroom, etc.

Notice the sights of this place ...
    the colors ...
    the shapes.

Notice the sounds of this place …
    the quiet …
    the wind …
    the birds …
    the heating system …
    the traffic outside your window.

Notice the temperature…
make sure it is perfect - not too hot and not too cold.
Notice how your body responds to this comfort.

Notice the smells.
If need be, bring any smell that you love to wherever you are.
You can have the smell of the ocean in a bedroom or the smell of vanilla in the forest.

And maybe, notice any taste.
What does the air taste like?
Or is there something in this space that you would like to taste?

Now, ask yourself if you would like having another being with you in that place.
It could be a person, a pet, a guide, an angel, a protector, an imaginary being, an ancestor, or any being that will bring you comfort.

If you wish, you can imagine that there is a barrier, or a shield, or a fence all around this place. It could be a physical barrier or it could be an energetic field. Because this is your place and it is in your mind, it can be anyway you want it. You can have a barrier above and below as well as around the perimeter of your place. Let yourself know that this is *your* place and no being can come in without your expressed permission. You can even put guards all around.

This is a place where you can always go to in your mind, just by remembering.

Holding the felt sense of this special place, gently begin to reconnect with your breath, feel your feet on the ground, your buttocks on the chair, couch or floor, and when you are ready, let yourself come back to this time and place.

You might want to draw, to write about, or to make a collage of this place to anchor it in your memory.

NOTES

Connecting with Nature

This meditation is best done outside. That being said, if you do not have easy access to the outside, you can work with a plant, by looking at the sky, or even with a picture of nature.

※ ※ ※

Induction

Find a quiet place to sit where you will be next to a natural element. It could be a flower, a plant, a tree, a lake, a mountain, etc.
Take your time and look at this natural object. If you can touch it, even better.

Let yourself be with that being.
What does it
look like…?
smell like…?
feel like…?

Let yourself connect with that being.
What is it telling you…
or showing you?

How does it feel being with this natural being?

What message does it have for you?

Remember that what you get is what you got, and that those messages sometimes do not come in complete sentences or make sense at the moment.

When you've spent as much time as you are ready to,
Return to your breath.
Breathing in... Breathing out.

Remember that you can reconnect with this experience any time you see that natural being, or practice it with any other natural being.

NOTES

Creating a Protective Shield

Many of us are highly sensitive to our ambiance, to the energy field around us. For some of us this can become overwhelming. This is particularly so if you find yourself around a lot of people or are in contact with negative people. This meditation is geared towards protecting you from being bombarded by other people's energy. It can be a sit-down practice or something that you do more casually on the spot when you are around lots of people. I tend to do it while in the shower in the morning, surrounding myself with a clean energy field that deflects any negative or too intense energy that I might encounter during the day. This energy field does not screen out loving or compassionate energy, either coming in, or going out.

❊ ❊ ❊

Induction

Imagine or visualize a protective shield surrounding you.
This shield can be made of some sort of material or it can simple be beams of energy.
Your shield can be solid or gauzy or mesh ...
it can light or heavy ...
it could be a bubble of light that surrounds you like a balloon...
or it could be a chainmail armor.

This shield has two unique qualities.

    a) It allows for all your positive energy to be directed towards others.

It also permits the entrance of any loving/healing/positive/caring energy that comes your way.
b) This shield prevents any negative/hurtful/mean/angry energy to come in.
If you chose, you can also bounce this negative energy back towards the person who sent it as love and healing.

Take a moment to feel yourself in this bubble of protection.

Let all your frightened, overwhelmed parts become aware of this protection. If any of your parts need extra protection, add anything that would make them feel even safer.

When you are ready, take your left hand and place it on the part of your body where you would like to store your shield. Note the sensation of feeling protected and safe. You can always reconnect to your shield by placing your hand on the part of your body where you placed it and remembering.

Maintaining that shield around you, let yourself come back to this time and place taking a couple of deep breaths.

How do you feel?

NOTES

Connecting with your True Self

There is a Hawaiian myth that says that when a child is born s/he/they is gifted with a beautiful bowl of Koa wood, filled with light. However, life happens and pebbles are thrown in, that slowly but surely begin to obscure the light until it is barely seen, if at all.

This happens to most of us. As we age we become increasingly removed from having access to the light that we are. This meditation guides you to reconnect with that light within.

❊ ❊ ❊

Induction

In your imagination, visualize a bowl filled it with pebbles. (This is also a powerful Ceremony - see Ceremonies, pg. 53)

In your mind's eye, pick up a pebble and name it with a negative belief that you hold about yourself.
Ask yourself how you took on that belief…?
Who told you were less than perfect…?
What decision did you make about life as a result of that belief…?

When you are ready, let go of it, knowing that it doesn't belong to you.
You might even return that belief to the person who gave it to you.

You can repeat this process for as long as you wish, with as many negative beliefs and decisions as you are ready to let go of at this time.

Now imagine seeing the light at the bottom of the bowl.
This is the true you, not all the junk that has been piled upon you.
Of course you are imperfect, we all are.
Yet, at core we are all beings of light, and the more you can connect to that sense of yourself, the more it will manifest on the outside.
That's how we change the world!

If it helps, think of someone you know, or know of, who exemplifies that essence.
It could be your relative, your neighbor, a character in a book or movie, or a spiritual leader.
And let yourself know that we all have the same core.

So shine on!

When you are ready, take a couple of deep breaths.
Breathing in…Breathing out.
Slowly, let yourself coming back to this moment, remembering that you are light and beauty.

NOTES

Letting Go of Negative Beliefs and ideas

This meditation is also quite effective as a Ceremony—see the Ceremonies section of this book.

❊ ❊ ❊

Induction

With kindness towards yourself, let yourself connect with any beliefs, any ideas, or any person that you know no longer serves you at this time in your life. Ask yourself which of these you are ready to let go of. (If you're not ready, don't push it, but ask yourself what prevents you from doing so.)

As you bring each person, idea, or belief to mind, imagine placing each of them in a beautiful colorful balloon that is attached to you by a cord.

When you feel ready, imagine taking a pair of scissors, or a knife, and cutting the ribbon that attaches this balloon filled with the belief, the idea, or the person that you are ready to release.

Once you have cut the ribbon, watch the balloon float up and away. As it moves further and further up feel yourself freer and freer of that belief, that idea, or that person.

Another possibility.

Visualize placing those negative beliefs, ideas, or people on a leaf or a stick. Imagine placing this leaf or this stick on a stream to be carried away by the current. As the leaf or stick floats away downstream feel those ideas, beliefs or persons floating away from you.

Another possibility.

You can imagine burying any negative beliefs, ideas or people deep into the earth.

Another possibility

Imagine these negative ideas, beliefs or persons being burned through in a sacred fire.

Once you feel done, thank all your parts for their willingness to do this.
Take a moment to acknowledge the work that you've done.
Take a couple of deep breaths...
Breathing in... breathing out.

When you feel ready come back to this time and place.

NOTES

Reclaiming Aspects or Parts of Yourself

Induction

Remember back to a time or times when you possessed certain parts or aspects of yourself that you feel that you have lost, buried or ignored. It could be a way that you felt, something you liked to do, an attitude, an innocence, a way of looking at things ...

Imagine those aspects of yourself.
How old were you?
What was it like to feel that way or do those things?
What happened that you stopped?
What prevents you now from being that way or doing that thing?

Imagine those parts, those aspects of yourself that have been set aside come back into your life.

Notice any changes in your physical, emotional and mental bodies as you reconnect with those parts of yourself that have been neglected, set aside, or buried for so many years.

Take your time ... allow yourself to reconnect and embrace those gifts or aspects of yourself that you had to discard and that have been missing.

Can you set the intention of allowing those parts to have more space in your life?

Be gentle and slow...

Recapture those aspects/parts of yourself one by one.
If you try to do it all at once, you will overwhelm your system.
Which can you begin re-implementing in your life?
Can you let the ones that you are not ready to put into action at this time know that you will endeavor to return to get them at a later time?

Now I invite you to give that part or aspect of yourself a sensation, or a shape, or a color and place your hand on a spot in your body in which you would like to store it. Or, you could just experience the warmth of your hand.

Every time you touch that part of your body practice calling to mind those reclaimed parts of yourself.

Acknowledge yourself for our willingness to reconnect with your lost parts.

Experience yourself as the amazing being that you are - remember the True Self meditation.

Take a couple of breaths.
Breathing in... Breathing out..
And when you are ready, let yourself come back to this time and space.

NOTES

Working with Loss

Loss is inevitable. This meditation offers a way to be with, and to assist, parts that hold loss in a way that allows you to be with those parts without becoming overwhelmed by them.

Induction

Gently allow yourself to get in touch with any part that holds feelings of loss.

It may be a recent loss, or one from long ago.
It may be the loss of a person, of an animal, of a situation, of a place or of a thing.

Allow yourself to simply BE - to be present - with those parts...
Honor their pain...
Witness their showing you what, or who, they are missing...
Recognize their anger...
Acknowledge their sadness...
Make room for any other feelings those parts hold.

Let those parts know that it is okay to have whatever feelings they have.

Ask those parts that have suffered the loss what they need from you. (this is not fixing)

Maybe they need understanding, or compassion, or loving kindness, or gentleness, or maybe they need you to perform some kind of action.

Agree, if you can, to undertake to give those parts what they need - even if only in your mind's eye.

Thank your parts for their courage in showing up.

When you are ready let yourself come back to this time. Breathing in... Breathing out.

NOTES

Being Other

Induction

Allow your mind to float back to the first time you became aware of being "other' ... not like.

How old were you?
What made you notice that you were 'other'?
Was it your gender?, your skin color?, your hair color?, your size?, your accent?, your clothes?, your parents?, your abilities?

Did you feel smarter, dumber, more athletic, clumsier, more beautiful, less attractive, etc.....?

What feelings did this discovery engender?

Connecting with the part that noticed being other, what did that part feel about itself then?
Was it a good feeling? Pride, excitement, power, joy, etc.
Or was it a not so good feeling? Shame, hurt, guilt, fear, etc.

What decisions did that part make about yourself and the world?

How have those beliefs and decisions helped you in your life...?
How have those beliefs and decisions hurt you in your life...?
Are those beliefs actually true...?
Do the decisions that sprung from them still make sense today?

Would that part like to change its world view or is it comfortable with how it is now?

What are the benefits from continuing the way it has been…?
What is lost by maintaining those beliefs and decisions…?
What benefit would there be in changing those beliefs and decisions…?
How would it impact your life to live from a different set of beliefs and decisions…?
What would you lose if you gave up these old ways of being?

Connecting with your greater wisdom, what would you like to tell the parts that took on those beliefs and made those decisions?

If the part that took on those beliefs and made those decisions would like to change, how would it like to do that?
Is that realistic or is it a fantasy?
Would it be kinder and wiser to accept yourself as you are, rather than trying to be someone other than who you are?

Thank your parts for showing you how the beliefs and decisions that you made early in your life have impacted you through out.

Return your attention to your breath.
Breathing in… Breathing out.
Gently let yourself come back to this time and place.

NOTES

Finding and Connecting with Guides and or Power Animals

There are many protocols to connect with angels, guides and power animals.

I like using this practice as a way to get clarity and guidance on issues that my mind can't figure out, or during those times when I'm too conflicted to have any wisdom about how to proceed.

If you already have a practice to do so, by all means follow your tradition. This meditation is a simple way to connect. In Shamanism, it is customary to use drumming when doing this type of meditation. You can google "shamanic drumming" and download one that feels right to you. Usually, the drumming for what is called a Journey is around 10-20 minutes. You can use "Centering Prayer" techniques. Another model is to use chants. Follow whatever model your personal tradition calls for. If you don't have a personal tradition to access Guides or Power Animals experiment until you find the one that suits you best. I find that this practice is a way to get clarity and guidance on issues that my mind can't figure out.

❊ ❊ ❊

Induction

Gently let yourself go inside and clear your mind.
Ask for a guide, a power animal, an angel, or an ancestor to come be with you.

You might see that being, or feel it or sense it (Each of us receives information differently.)

This being (or beings) might be one that is familiar to you or it might be a being who is coming to visit you on this particular occasion. You might even be visited by more than one being.

Welcome this being.
Thank it for showing up.
Spend a little time with that being, enjoying being together.

If you have a specific intention for connecting with this being, share your question or concern. Ask your being what wisdom it has for you.
What advice does it have to offer you?
Remember, answers don't always come as a narrative. You may receive information in images, in a symbolic way or in a cryptic way. If you do not understand the message, ask for clarification.

Take your time to have a dialogue with your guide, your angel, your ancestor, your power animal or whoever showed up.

When you feel as complete as you can be in this instance, let yourself come back to this time and place.

Breathing in... Breathing out.

NOTES

Being with Your Self

This meditation is geared to facilitating your connection with your higher wisdom in order to answer a question or get insight into a situation that you are finding challenging.

❋ ❋ ❋

Induction

    Gently go inside and connect with your higher Self, your Wisdom, or your Knowing.

Take your time to really connect with that energy.
When you are ready, ask whatever question your heart is yearning to know…
Do not be attached to a particular answer…
Let yourself be curious and open to whatever you receive …
opening to what wants to be shown to you, not necessarily what you want it to be.

Allow the answer to come from your heart and from your Knowing.
It might come as a picture, as a thought, as a feeling, or as a felt sense.
Trust that whatever you're gifted with, is what you need to know.

Thank your Self, your Wisdom, or your Knowing for its message.

Return your attention to your breathing.
Breathing in... Breathing out.
And when you are ready, let yourself come back to this reality.

NOTES

CEREMONIES

Creating Rituals for a Troubled World

Ceremony. When we've lost that, we've lost everything, and are only wandering in the dark, like chickens or lambs waiting for eagles.
—Rick Bass

INTRODUCTION

I have been fortunate to spend time with indigenous tribes that have been only marginally impacted by our Western civilization. They still live mostly as they did hundreds of years ago. As a whole they seem happier and less stressed than we are. They seem to have the capacity to take one day at a time. As it comes. One thing, among others, that touched me is their connection to Ceremony. It could be the way they serve you a drink, or the way they initiate a child into adulthood or acknowledge a completion of a training, or the way they honor the events of their every day life as well as the 'big' events like births and deaths.

As with the meditations in this book, the impulse for this book came from my supervisees and students who asked me where I got the ideas for the Ceremonies that I suggested they use with their clients—and themselves. I was always a bit shy and embarrassed to say that I had just made them up on the spot. Of course my suggestions were informed by many readings, by some of my teachers, by Ceremonies in the Shamanic practices that I was gifted to attend and by a number of my clients with whom Ceremonies were co-created to mark an event in their lives.

My first such client, whom I will call Mary, was talking about having had a miscarriage 35 years ago and feeling that there had never been closure. No funeral. No wake. No remembrance. As if it had never happened. Together we decided that it would be helpful to create a Ceremony of some sort to mark the event. We discussed a variety of possibilities and finally came up with the idea of a burial. She bought a few items that, to her, represented the loss of this child. Then we went to the woods, dug a hole, lit a candle and she buried those items. After that she planted a couple of seeds so that flowers would grow in that spot.

Originally, like the Meditations book, this book was written for my supervisees and other clinicians. However, as I received feedback from them on how their clients responded positively and wanted to find out more, I realized that I wanted to make ir available to anyone who is interested in ceremonializing some event in their life. It could be an actual event, a change of attitude, a new way of looking at the world, a time of transition, a letting go, or a beginning.

The feedback has been so positive that I am delighted to share it in this new format. In that spirit, the Ceremonies offered here are templates for you to create your own Ceremony, or to co-create one with family, colleagues, friends, and clients.

Some Ceremonies are best done with someone to hold space - be a witness - for you. That person can be a therapist, a coach, a spiritual teacher, or a loved one.

Other Ceremonies you might prefer to do on your own.

Whichever way you chose, make sure that you give yourself enough time to prepare and to perform the Ceremony. Preparation and execution do not have to be on the same day. Some Ceremonies require a lot of planning. Also make sure to include time to integrate after the Ceremony, either by yourself by writing or drawing, or by talking to someone you trust.

NOTES

NOTE FOR CLINICIANS

Inasmuch as this book originated with my work as a therapist, many of the Ceremonies offered here are connected with healing, for helping a part externalize the inner work. However, it also includes Ceremonies for rejoicing, acknowledging and accepting.

There are many, many different types of ceremonial practices that are helpful in healing psyche and body. As a therapist, there are some that I am comfortable doing within the therapeutic relationship, others not. When it does not feel appropriate for me to perform or to participate in the Ceremony because it would interfere with the therapeutic relationship, I explore with my client who in their circle might serve that role. I also often refer to people with whom I have worked who specialize in Ceremonies.

My intention is to share those Ceremonies that I have found helpful both for myself and my clients.

There are times in which my client and I will do the Ceremony in my office. Sometimes it is appropriate for me to participate (whether in my office or out of the office), other times I see my role as holding space and witnessing.

Most of the Ceremonies I offer here were gifted to me by my main teachers, Ipupiara & Claicha, who are Shamans from the Brazilian Amazon, from Gunilla Norris who taught me how to make the mundane sacred, and from the many people with whom I have co-created Ceremonies for specific events in their lives.

Most Ceremonies are quite simple, although of course, some can become quite elaborate.

There are many experiences that are enhanced by, acknowledged by, or honored by, Ceremony.

Ceremonies can be performed to acknowledge:

- Beginnings, transitions, or endings
- Bringing in and Letting Go
- Losses
- Celebrations

Ceremonies are different from rituals. Rituals are acts that we perform over and over. Rituals can be sacred: connecting with the Divine, or secular: brushing your teeth. Ceremonies on the other hand are a one-time event that is created and performed for a singular occasion. Although they are not necessarily spiritual or religious, they are sacred. For example a new job, a graduation, a change of attitude, a new world view, or a death.

In most cultures, including our own, Ceremonies are proscribed and the participant enters them following the protocols that have been established.

This is a good thing.

However, particularly in our Western culture, many of these Ceremonies have lost the depth of their meaning. I believe that the reason is, in part, that we have become a consumer focused culture.

In Ceremonies for Healing, we explore ways to co-create the Ceremonies with our clients so that they have a direct input into the deep meaning of the actions taken. The guide - you - and the participant, together, explore and decide the event to be ceremonialized. Then, again together, you plan how to best execute the Ceremony.

The reason behind including Ceremonies in a psychotherapy frame is that by doing so, we acknowledge, honor, and concretize completions, severances, incorporations, and transitions.

In concretizing the emotional work that has occurred, is occurring, or is about to occur, we anchor the work, moving from the pre-frontal cortex understanding (left brain) to feeling/doing (right brain) bringing about a holistic longer lasting impact.

In creating a Ceremony, the most important ingredients are *intention* and *attention*. My teachers always said that it's not so much *what* you do, but *how* you do it. In a Ceremony, every act is imbued with the quality and the intention for that Ceremony.

Some questions to ask:

- Why are we doing this Ceremony?
- Who needs to be involved?
- When should it be done?
- Where should it be done?
- What are the elements that will make this event a Ceremony?

NOTES

Setting

At the beginning of many of the Ceremony instructions, there is a reminder to be mindful of *Setting*. This refers to When? Where? How? Who?

Usually it is important to allow enough time to plan the Ceremony and bring it to fruition. This allows for you to be thoughtful about the Ceremony you are to perform and helps deepen the experience. Especially in our rush/busy world, taking the time to reflect and to do something slowly, with attention and intention, is a Ceremony in and of itself.

Find a time and a place where you will not be disturbed. Turn off all your electronics. Create an environment that feels special for you by using scents, candles, music, etc.

Determine whether you want to do this particular Ceremony on your own or whether you want to include other people. If you chose to include other people, be clear about what you expect from them. Do you want them to participate in some way or to quietly be witnesses? Ask ahead of time. Be clear about what you want and what you don't want. If that person cannot do what you ask, that can be disappointing but at least you will know in advance and can go to plan B.

Letting go Ceremonies are traditionally performed at dawn, or right after, full moon: Waning time. Bringing in Ceremonies are customarily done at dawn, or right after, new moon: Waxing time.

Occasionally in a psychotherapy, or a coaching session, or when listening deeply to someone, Ceremonies can occur spontaneously and be brief. At those time it is the attention and the intention with which the act is done that differentiates this act from an ordinary act. Offering someone a flower, a rock, a thing in your office, the bracelet you were wearing, a quote, etc. with intention can be a powerful Ceremony.

Many of the Ceremonies offered here are generic. They can be performed for a variety of purposes. It is the *intention* for that Ceremony that determines what it symbolizes. I also offer some Ceremonies that are geared to specific events in your life.

In all Ceremonies:

- Prepare the *setting* (this phrase will be used as the reminder for all Ceremonies).
- Remember to place your intention into the Ceremony you are performing.
- Be clear about what you want to accomplish.
- Give yourself enough time.
- Disconnect all your electronics.
- Find a private, safe place to do your Ceremony.
- Bring all the elements that you need for that particular Ceremony.

NOTES

Materials Used in Ceremonies

I prefer using simple materials that can be found rather than purchased. On the other hand, buying certain objects that have a particular relevance is wonderful as well.

I also often suggest connecting to the four elements—Earth, Water, Fire, and Air—in some way.

In many of the Ceremonies that I offer, there is a suggestion of burying, burning, or placing an object in water. I also suggest that those elements be in some way present in the space where you are having the Ceremony. It doesn't have to be fancy or complicated. You can use a small bowl of water, a candle, a plant, and a rock.

That being said, I believe that it is important to honor and follow your personal spiritual practices, if you have them. For example, Carla, who is Christian, went to Church and burned candles to the Blessed Mother to ask for a clearing of the energy of having been raped. Alexa, from a Buddhist tradition, burned incense and sprinkled essences around her apartment to honor the good feelings and the joy she was beginning to experience. Roland and Sarah went into the woods and buried seeds to bring fertility into their lives. Jim bought flowers to celebrate his positive attitude and to welcome his new found happiness. Mary bought baby items and buried them to acknowledge and honor the miscarriage she had had.

Stones, shells, or other small objects.

Imbuing the object.

These are particularly valuable to anchor an accomplishment, or a good feeling, or as a reminder of a new thought, or of an action to be carried through.

For example you could say something like: I'd like to imbue this stone with the feeling of safety, happiness, joy, peace, or love that I'm feeling at this moment. Whenever you feel this stone, let yourself recapture the feeling with which you imbued the stone.

George imbued his stone with gentleness; Laura imbued hers with a sense of power.

Sticks, yarn and ribbons.

You will note that these are called for in many of the Ceremonies that are offered in the following pages. They can be used on their own or in combination with other items. They are used for both Bringing In and Letting Go Ceremonies.

Wrapping a stick.

This Ceremony is recommended for both "Letting Go" and "Bringing in". It can be wonderfully healing to do both consecutively. However, let yourself be the judge of what is best for you. You may want to have some time to process the "Letting Go," before you perform the "Bringing In." I personally like to do both within a short period of time as I feel that I want to replace what I'm releasing with something positive.

You may use one stick or two.

It is preferable to use a branch from a tree or bush rather than a piece of plywood (but use what you can—remember that the intention is what matters most.)

Balloons.

Balloons can be used for either Bringing In or Letting Go Ceremonies.

Get one balloon or a bunch if you prefer. What matters is that if it feels right to you. You can pick different sizes, colors, and shapes.

Set the intention of what you want to Bring In or Let Go of—not both in the same bunch. If you chose to let go and bring in at the same time, do each Ceremony sequentially, so it is clear which one you are doing.

You can Let Go or Bring In an attitude, a job, a person, a belief, etc.

Imbue the balloons with what you want to release or receive. You can do that by writing on the balloons, or putting stickers on them, or decorating them in any way that calls to you. Use your imagination. What you do cannot be too simple or too ornate. What matters is that it be meaningful to you and that you take the time and concentration to do it.

When you feel ready, release the balloons into the air and watch them float away asking for your desire to be heeded and fulfilled.

Paper, pencils, pens, markers, paint.

These are very handy to have and can be used for almost any Ceremony you want to create.

Drumming, rattling and music.

Drumming, rattling and other music making are used in indigenous culture to maintain the connection to the present moment while a Ceremony is being performed.

You can play music you like, or listen to a recording., You can also ask someone to play some music, recite a poem, or sing a song. It matters that it be music that is meaningful to you, not what the people who are playing it think is 'right.'

Candles, essences, incense.

These items are traditionally used to create mood. Chose any that appeal to you.

Power Animals, Angels, Guides.

In Shamanism, power animals assist us in connecting with information that is usually unavailable to our conscious mind. Other traditions call upon angels, guides, protectors or Higher Self. They are also a source of comfort and support. Although each tradition has its own philosophical beliefs, I find that for the purpose of creating a Ceremony and calling in higher beings, whatever fits your particular views, is what is right for you.

Following is one way to go on a shamanic journey. There are many.

You can either have someone drum for you - if they know shamanic drumming - or listen to a shamanic journey drumming podcast which you can easily find on youtube.

It is best to lie down. Close your eyes, relax your body, uncross your arms and your legs.

Take a few deep breaths.

Imagine a way to go down into the earth. You can use a hole in the ground, or follow the roots of a tree, or go down a manhole, or take an elevator to underground, etc.

Slowly let yourself descend into the earth...

Notice what you see/feel/smell...

Shortly, you arrive at a body of water that is just right for you - not too hot, not too cold, not too deep.

Find a way to get across the water and when you arrive to the other shore an animal (or being) will be waiting for you.

Ask if s/he is your power animal or being guide.

If not, ask to be taken to your power animal or guide.

When you meet your power animal or being, connect with her/him. When you feel ready, ask that being the question that you have come to ask, or any request that you have for that being.

Wait for their answer. It might take a little while. Remember that the message might come in images, or scents, or knowing, not necessarily in words.

After a few minutes (usually between 7 and 20 minutes) the beat of the drum will change as a signal that it is time to come back to this reality.

Thank your helper for connecting with you. Begin you return - across the water, up through the same way as you went down, until you arrive back to this time and place.

Breathe in ... Breathe out.

Another technique is to do a visualization meditation and follow the basic same steps of imagining yourself going to another place to meet the being that is there to assist you with your issue or question.

If you are doing Centering Prayer, repeat the word or words that you typically use to connect.

Use any practice with which you are familiar and comfortable.

NOTES

Letting Go Ceremonies

The following pages offer several "Letting Go" Ceremonies.

The framework for these Ceremonies is loose and a variety of elements can be combined. The suggestions offered in this book can be used as is, or can be used as a springboard for your own creation, depending on the situation and your desires.

It is important though to remember that none of this is magic! (Though some would like to believe it is.) What those Ceremonies do is to create, or anchor, a desire to be cleared of negativity, of bad feelings, of hurts, of resentments, or of any burden that we carry about things that we have done, or not done, or have been done to us. (Note that this is in no way condoning negative/hurtful behavior from someone else, but it is a desire to be free of the burden we carry as a result.)

I really like Clarrissa Pinkola Estes description of Forgiveness. Paraphrased it is that forgiveness is letting go of the burden of resentment we carry for what was done to us.

NOTES

LETTING GO OF NEGATIVE ENERGY

Carrying Negative Energy is like drinking
poison hoping the other person will die.
St. Augustine seems to have been the first to say this quote

Burying, Gifting to the Waters, or Burning

These "Letting Go" ceremonies are beneficial when there has been incomplete mourning. It can be the loss of a person, of a thing, of an idea, of an illusion, of a possibility, of a situation, etc.

Find some item(s) that belonged to, represent or are symbolic of the person, the idea, the thing or the situation you are ready to release. You can also use pen and paper to write or draw what you are letting go of.

Setting

Find a spot in a park or a backyard and literally bury the items that you have brought.

Another option is to go to a body of water and ask the body of water to receive the item, or items, that you are wanting to give up.

Still another option is to make a fire and burn the items you have prepared for the occasion.

These Ceremonies can easily be done on your own. However, you can always ask supportive others to be with you.

After you are done with the Ceremony, it is helpful and healing to find and acknowledge the gift, or the teaching, from the experience that you just release even though it may have been a difficult one.

You might acknowledge your strength, your capacity for joy, your resilience …

NOTES

Baths

I wish to offer two types of baths. The first is for every day maintenance. The second is for healing wounds of abuse, particularly physical abuse.

Under-rated in our culture, baths are an excellent way to let go of the stress. If you do not have access to a bathtub, an extended warm shower will do the trick. Draw a warm bath and as you soak, let your body release all the stress, all the tension, all the hurrying and worrying that you have accumulate during the day. Adding Sea Salt or Epsom Salt is recommended as well. Feel free to use oils and essences to enhance the experience. A warm bath or shower is also a lovely aid for those of you who have difficulties falling asleep.

Baths are traditionally used for clearing the energy of any kind of physical abuse. I have found that it is of great help to people who have been violated through rape, sexual abuse, incest, or any other form of physical abuse.

Setting.

The more time-honored way is to take the bath in a natural setting such as sacred body of water like a river, a lake, or the ocean. You might choose to bring some herbs or plants to rub on your body to help release any negative energy. Some traditions believe that the ocean is best because the saline composition of the water is considered an exceptional energy clearer. (if you do not have access to an ocean, you can use sea salt.) Do what is easily feasible, rather than postpone to get the exact "right" setting. Remember intention, intention!

In the Amazon Jungle, a bath is done by having a bucket of water with herbs in it doused on your head.

When you are done give thanks to the waters and the herbs for taking on any negativity and transmuting it.

If you do not have easy access to a body of water, use your bathtub or even a shower *(More information about that later on.)*

If you are conducting the Ceremony outdoors, make sure to bring some towels or a blanket to wrap yourself in after you come out of the water, so you do not get chilled. A hot beverage, like tea, is both warming and soothing You may choose to anoint your cleared self with oils, perfumes, etc. It can be nourishing to have someone hold space, or be a witness for you, to welcome the new you out of the water, and to be the one to pamper you with towels, oils, perfumes and tea.

Natalie gathered a few of her women friends. Together, they went down to the lake at full moon. She bathed herself in the waters and asked that any of the energy of her perpetrator be removed from her and transmuted by the waters (This is the letting go part.) Then her friends anointed her with lovely oils and lotions saying things like: "This is your pure, beautiful, magnificent body that belongs to you" (This is the bringing in part.)

If you are using a bath tub, you might want to create an environment of sacredness by lighting candles, burning incense, playing music, or anything else that feels special to you. You can put 1 cup of sea salt, or herbs, or both. Again you may ask someone to serve as witness.

Lastly, you can use a shower if none of the above is available to you for whatever reason. The best way to do this is the following. You set up as before: candles, etc. Then take a container that is not metal. Fill it 1/3 with sea salt and 2/3 with warm water so it dissolves. You can use other herbs as well, if you so wish. When in the shower, pour the salt, or herbed water, over yourself and ask your body to release any negative energy that it holds.

NOTES

Using a stick and yarn, ribbons, thread, grass or anything that can be used for wrapping

Setting.

Get a stick. Any stick will do. It can be small or big, smooth or rough, have branches or not.

It is best to use a stick that you find in nature rather than one you buy at a hardware store, but use what you can.

Gather colored ribbons, or yarn, or anything that can be wrapped. You can use many colors or just one; use your imagination and what seems to correspond to what you are planning to release.

Wrap the stick with your wrapping material and let each turn represent the person, the event, the belief, or the issue you are wanting to let go of. It could be different aspects of the same issue, or it could be different people connected to an event, or different times in which the situation occurred. It is preferable to focus on one issue at a time. However, including many aspects of one issue or event helps with the clearing.

For example, if you are working with shame, you could wrap the stick with each time shame was felt or with each person who shamed you.

Feel free to insert words, pictures, or small objects into the wrap.

You can repeat the issue, person, belief, etc., several times as you wrap the stick. Each time, letting the memories and the feelings connected to that event or issue go into the yarn.

Once you have wrapped the stick to your satisfaction (it can be done in one sitting or you can come back to it several times until you feel finished) decide how you want to dispose of your stick. I prefer to use a natural way of releasing the energy that has been transferred to the wrapping material and the stick. This is where the use of the four elements comes into play again.

My suggestions are to burn the stick, to bury it, or to gift it to the waters.

One my clients chose a dumpster -so choose whatever feels right to you. (you can't do it wrong.)

Connect with the element that you choose to dispose of the stick. Ask that element to take any negative energy with which it has been imbued. Request that that negative energy be transmuted into something positive. For example, if you had been working with shame, you might ask for self-confidence, for freedom, or whatever the opposite of shame would be for you.

When you are done, thank the elements for taking on the negative energy and transforming it into a positive.

Miriam started wrapping her stick with wanting to let go of the shame of having been "fat" as a child. As she wrapped she became in touch with all the ways she had been shamed for her body and the beliefs that she took on about herself as a result. She realized, among other things, how she hated her body. The process took a long time. There were tears and anger and hurt. When she finished, Miriam broke the stick into pieces and burned it, releasing into the ether the shame and beliefs that had hurt her for so many years.

Later on, Miriam did a Ceremony of reclaiming her body and began a new healthy, loving, relationship with herself.

NOTES

Writing and/or drawing

Setting.

Take a clean piece of paper and write, draw, paint, make a collage of, or any combination of all those to represent whatever you are ready to let go.

You can connect this with the above stick wrapping exercise and include the words, pictures etc., in the wrapping fibers.

This can be done as a one time sequence, or over time, coming back to it at intervals.

Like the stick, you can dispose of the writing or drawing by burning it, burying it, or gifting it to the waters. You can also cut or shred the paper before you discard it.

Again, ask that the negative energy, idea, or belief that you are shedding be transformed into a positive energy. Reclaim the beauty and the strength that was taken away by those beliefs and ideas.

NOTES

Casting off

Setting.

This Ceremony is taken from the Jewish Ceremony of Tashlikh, which means to cast off. It is an ancient practice that is performed on the afternoon before the night of Rosh-ha-Shana (new year). In that Ceremony, one throws bread into a body of water to cleanse one's sins from the year that has been, so as to enter the new year pure. Other spiritual tradition, have their own rituals of casting off.

Traditionally, Tashlikh is about casting off one's sins. However, the way I interpret it, is that it is also an opportunity to let go of any thoughts, any regrets, any decisions, any beliefs, any resentments, any hurts, any grief, any anger, or any negative feeling that prevent us from feeling fully alive and happy.

The Jewish custom is to use bread crumbs that have been imbued with whatever we are shedding. The crumbs are then thrown into the water. If bread crumbs don't feel right for you, feel free to use whatever does feel right. You can use grains of rice, petals of flowers, twigs, small stones, etc. Just be sure that anything you cast into the water will not be harmful to the beings living there.

As you throw your objects into the water ask that this belief, this idea, this resentment, or whatever you are ready to release, be removed from every cell of your physical, emotional and mental bodies so that you may be free.

Give thanks to the water for taking your negativity and transmuting it into food and positive energy.

My personal favorite way to cast off is to go to the beach, gather some rocks and pebbles from the sand and hurl them into the surf while yelling at the top of my lung all the things I want to give up. It is very cathartic for me to be able to be forceful and to have the sound of the surf absorb my pain, my anger, my hurt, or any other emotion I'm dealing with at the time.

When I'm done venting and throwing, I take some of the water and pour it over my head and my body to clear and renew me. Then I thank the waters for their generosity.

NOTES

Making a water vessel

Setting.

This Ceremony was gifted to me by a client who had spent a long time in India and watched Ceremonies along the Ganges.

Make a little boat or a platform with balsam wood (easily found in craft stores) or you can use a leaf or anything light enough and yet strong enough to hold a tea candle.

Place anything that you want to let go of into the candle. Place the lit candle on the little boat or the leaf. Place the boat on the moving water and watch it flow down away from you. As it floats away, let yourself feel freer and more distant from what you placed in the candle.

When it disappears, give thanks to the candle and to the water. Feel the distance between you and those feelings, those ideas and those beliefs that you were able to give up.

NOTES

LETTING GO OF NEGATIVE ATTACHMENTS AND CONNECTIONS TO OTHER PEOPLE

Severing negative strings of connection.

Setting.

Many of us have conflictual relationship/feelings with the people in our lives. We love them and have resentments, hurts, anger, pain, and other negative feelings connected to them. Those people may be close to us physically. They may be distant, yet they linger as part of our lives. They may be alive or they might be dead.

As long as we continue to carry negative feelings towards other people, we are weighed down by those feelings, whether they know it or not. We cannot be completely free. The following Ceremonies are designed to free you from those burdens. Possibly it will help heal the relationship, if that is what you wish and what is meant to be. However, it doesn't have to be so. You may choose to totally sever the connection to that person. Severing the connection completely might be a good outcome.

Using the stick and ribbon technique described above.

As you wrap your stick with ribbons, yarn, thread or whatever you chose, name the connections you wish to sever. You can name the person or you can name the negative cord that ties you to that person. You can use different colors for different people or, if you prefer, you can repeat the process for different people or separate issues. As you wrap your yarn or ribbon, you can write the person(s) name, the issue you're working with, the connection you want to sever and embed those into the wrapping.

When you feel complete break the stick, symbolically breaking the ties to these individuals. When you feel ready, burn the stick, offer it to the waters, or give it to mother earth asking that element to transmute and clear the negative energies which it collected.

Finish your Ceremony by do a loving kindness meditation towards yourself regaining any freedom that you lost carrying these ties. Later on, if you feel up to it, do a loving kindness meditation towards those you have released.

Using ribbons, yarn, sweet grass, etc. - different from the above

Gather a bunch of ribbons, yarns, sweet grass, ropes or any other weaving material in as many textures and colors as you feel called to collect.

Begin braiding these strands, mentioning the name of those people with whom you feel you have a negative connection. Continue braiding until you feel complete, at least for now.

Then cut up the braid in as many pieces as feels right, saying to yourself: "I free myself from this negative connection, I let you go." After you're done with the cutting, burn the fragments, bury them, or place them into a body of water asking that the energy that they carry be changed and cleared.

Once you are done, take some time to bring back into yourself any positive attributes, gifts, energies, beliefs, or attitudes that you had to give up to stay connected to those people.

There are many ways to do this:
You can name those positive qualities...
You can braid a bracelet with the positives...
You can write a few lines...
You can draw, paint etc.

Sam wanted to let go of the string he felt kept him attached to an old relationship that had been hurtful and demeaning and in some way kept him from entering into a new more positive relationship. He did a letting go Ceremony, and to celebrate he went to get hot chocolate and cake as a statement of his freedom to do whatever he wanted.

NOTES

Bringing in Ceremonies

Bringing in Ceremonies use the same materials and often the same actions as the Letting Go Ceremonies. That is because one of the main ingredients of a Ceremony is *purpose*, and the *manner* in which the Ceremony is performed.

Just like the Letting Go Ceremonies, these can easily take a couple of hours to perform and it might take a few days to gather the materials, find the right space, and set aside the right time.

Again it is important to remember that Ceremonies are not magic. However, they do open the energy channels for change to happen.

As in all Ceremonies, make sure you create an environment (*setting*) that is conducive and propitious to the intent that you are inviting in your Ceremony.

The more specific you can be for any given Ceremony, the better. For example, if you want to bring a partner into your life, be specific as to what type of partner you are looking for. One of my clients wanted a male romantic partner who would share her views of life. So she asked for a partner and manifested a wonderful female business partner. She was pleased with the outcome, though annoyed that it wasn't what she really wanted. Another client asked for bundance in his life. He wasn't clear about what abundance meant to him. So he doubled his net worth, but what he wanted was relationships, friendships, connections.

Be clear. You can do as many Ceremonies as you wish over time.

NOTES

Using sticks, ribbons, yarn, thread, sweetgrass etc.

This is similar to the Letting Go technique,. However this time the intention is to Bring In.

A word of caution... Do not ask for too many things at once. That will dilute the intention. Better to ask for one or two things that are really important to you. Then let some time pass before you ask for the next thing.

Setting.

Find a stick that you like. Preferably one from nature.

Using yarn, ribbons, threads, sweetgrass or rope, wrap the stick naming those things that you want to bring into your life. You can use different colors or materials for different things, or just put your intention into the one strand that you are working with.

You can also write words, or use pictures, or find small objects to weave into the wrapping with the things that you want to bring in. It is important to only ask for positive things. I am told the universe does not understand negatives, so make sure that you phrase what you want into positive language. For example ask for a new place to live, not to be rid of the one you have. Also it is suggested that you be precise and detailed in what you ask. A new place to live could be a tent!

Do not ever ask for something negative to happen to someone else. That only spreads negative energy and that is not what you want to bring into your life.

You can ask for very specific personal things, or for bigger global happenings such as world peace. You can ask for material things. You can request changes in attitude, wish for a different view point, or invite new ideas, or beliefs.

When you feel complete, you may wish to keep the stick around for a while as a reminder of your desire. Reinforcing the wish that it be granted to you.

When you feel the time is right, burn the stick, bury it, or gift it to the waters asking those elements to carry your desires out into the universe to be manifested.

I also like using the phrase "this or something better." Do not limit yourself.

When you are done, give thanks for that which is already yours.

NOTES

Using flowers

Setting.

This is very similar to the Ceremony using a stick. The difference is that you are using a bundle of flowers instead of a stick. In the tradition that I learned, they use roses. However, I have also heard of other flowers or plants. So my suggestion is that you use whatever flower is calling to you and is available.

According to my teachers Ipupiara & Claicha use:
Pink for matters of the heart
Red for abundance
White for clarity

As in the stick technique, use strands of varied materials to wrap your desires into the stems of the flowers that you have gathered. You can insert words or small objects into the wrap.

When you are finished with the wrapping, place the bunch of flowers upside down in a place where no one but you can see it for a week, (in your closet if necessary) asking for your desires to be noted and fulfilled.

They also taught that it is best to do it on a Tuesday or a Friday.

After the week is over, gift the bundle to the waters, bury it, or burn it giving thanks for that which you are about to receive.

Shairy, one of my teachers, suggests that you give thanks for what you have already received, giving the message that it is inevitable for you to get what you ask for. He however cautions that certain things are not to be granted. A bit of a catch 22.

NOTES

Creating a vision board

This exercise has become more popular over the last few years. Nonetheless, it is a very powerful practice. It is believed that it allows your unconscious to formulate and visualize that which you want to bring into your life.

You can create a vision board for something concrete: a job, a relationship, a place to live, or anything you want to bring into your life. You can also create a board for something less tangible: an attitude, a world view, a situation, or an aspiration.

Typically vision boards are done over time. This way, you can add details and other elements as your vision expands. That being said, you can also create a vision board in one sitting, just give yourself enough time.

Setting.

Gather a large piece of card board, of oak tag, of heavy paper, of balsam wood, of presentation board, or any stiff material that appeals to you. Make sure that the board you chose will accept the elements you will use to create the image. Typical are: paint, ink, paste, cut outs from magazines, paper with words, and sometimes things from nature. You may also need things like scissors, push pins, and sticky tape.

Decorate your board in a way that is pleasing to you. Feel free to use representations that are concrete or ones that are symbolic for you.

You can do one board and include many things, or several boards to represent different aspects of that which you are wanting to bring in. For example, a board for work, a board for love, a board for travel, etc.

When you feel done, give thanks for having all those things in your life already. Then place the board where you will see it often. This is a reminder of the intention that you have put into it. Some people believe that it is best to make the vision board and then just put it away and not look at it for a while - maybe a year.

When one of the desires that you placed on your board becomes a reality for you (not always in the way that you expected) acknowledge it and give thanks for it.

Another approach is to take the board and burn it, or bury it, or gift to the waters asking the elements to take your request and make it manifest.

NOTES

Gathering

This Ceremony is deceptively simple

Setting.

With the intention of what you want to bring into your life, gather some items that are representative of your request. You can gather items found around your home, outside in nature and in shops.

What matters is not the artifacts themselves, but what each means to you. What is the essence, the quality, that this item symbolizes for you. It could be a twig, a statue, a seed, a coin, a book, or a sweater.

Create an "altar" (a special spot) and place your objects on it. You can use a portion of your window ledge, a corner of your desk, a space on your vanity, or a more elaborate setting. The important part is that the items be pleasing and comfortable for you. It doesn't matter that it "look" a certain way. I have mini altars with rocks and small items all over my living space. They may not conform to what an "altar" should look like, but I like them and they are meaningful to me.

If possible, position your altar in a spot that you pass often and where they will not be disturbed by others. If that is not possible because of your particular living situation, you can create a portable "altar" by placing your items in a small pouch that you can have in your bag or pocket.

Every time you notice your "altar" remember your intention.

Another approach is to take your items and burn them, bury them, or gift them to the waters asking the elements to take your request and grant it to you.

Give thanks.

NOTES

Little Boat

Like the previous Ceremony, this technique seems almost unimportant. Yet when done with attention and intention, it is quite powerful.

Setting.

This Ceremony is similar to the one for Letting Go. The difference is that this time you are wishing to Bring In.

Make a little boat or platform with a piece of wood, a leaf or any material that appeals to you that will float for at least a little while.

Place a tea candle, a symbolic small object, a piece of writing, an image or a drawing on the little boat with your request for what you want to bring into your life.

Set it afloat on a body of water asking for that which you want to bring into your life. Watch it move until it disappears. Thank the waters for carrying your wish.

NOTES

Creating a Treasure Box

One of my favorites is to create a treasure box, or a special envelope, or a discrete file. I encourage you to make it concrete rather than having a file on your computer. There is something energetic about having something that is concrete rather than virtual. Yet, it is your special container... use what feels authentic to you.

You can buy a special box, or you can use any box that you own and like, or use an old box and decorate it.

Setting.

In your box, place any accolade, any card, any word of praise, or any good wish that you have received. Many of us have a tendency to either dismiss, or forget, the good that comes to us.

When someone gives you a compliment or sends you a special note, put it in the box. When you want to celebrate and remember a part that has grown or changed, that has become freer, happier, or stronger, etc. write it down and put it in the box. Allow yourself to accumulate the positives that come your way. This is not bragging... it's acknowledging!

When you feel bad, or start doubting yourself, open the box and remind yourself of all the positiveness that you've garnered.

NOTES

SPECIFIC CEREMONIES

WORKING WITH LOSS

Eyes that do not cry, do not see.
—Swedish proverb

Dealing with a miscarriage, an abortion, or giving up a child.

Our culture typically does not acknowledge the emotional and psychological impact of the loss of an unborn child. There is no ritual, no rite of passage, no societal recognition of the event. Even most hospital staff see it as just another procedure. When someone dies, we have Ceremonies to mark the passing. Those vary depending on the culture, the background and the spiritual affiliation of those who are left to grieve. Although they are quite different in the way they are executed, all these Ceremonies have in common a recognition of loss and what it might mean to those suffering it. Most grieving Ceremonies are designed to bring comfort and community to the mourners.

In the case of a miscarriage, there is no such thing. Most miscarriages are very private matters. Most women never even talk about it, except maybe with very close members of their inner circle. No Ceremony, no burial, no community to support and to comfort. After a visit to the doctor, there is an expectation that the person suffering the loss should go back to their life as usual, as if nothing happened. For women (and some men) who have suffered several miscarriages, there may also be a feeling of failure or hopelessness.

This lack of support is often even greater for women who have had an abortion. For many there is the added sense of shame or guilt. Shame and/or guilt for having gotten pregnant in the first place, shame and/or guilt for choosing to end the pregnancy. Also quite often, the woman has to go get the procedure on her own - alone. Some facilities endeavor to help ease the pain. Many do not, and women are treated like just another body. In some cases there is even some subtle (or not so subtle) disapproval of their actions.

Additionally, it is important to note that although the death of an unborn child happens physically to women, men are impacted as well.

The loss of having had to give up a live child for adoption is seldom mentioned, even in the literature. Giving a child up for adoption puts the biological parent in a state that Pauline Boss calls 'ambiguous loss.' The person is lost to you, yet still exists. So they are there and not there. When someone has to give a child away, that child is still present in their memory/psyche, even if they didn't spend any time with the child. There is the wonder of where, with whom, and how is that child. What is s/he like? etc. This situation makes things emotionally more difficult as there is no clear closure. Perhaps the hope that they will meet at some point still lingers. In those cases I recommend that what is grieved is the loss of the opportunity, the loss of being with that child, the loss of the opportunity to have been a parent, even if other children ensue.

The Ceremonies offered here are for both partners, if they so choose. Performing the Ceremony together can bring a sense of shared grief and closeness and may allow each person to speak that which is often difficult to verbalize.

Unfortunately, that is not always the case and quite often the woman must grieve and heal on her own. In those cases I highly recommend that the grieving person gather those who will be able to comfort her and support her as she performs the Ceremony of Letting Go.

NOTES

Ceremony for an Unborn Child

I offer many steps to this Ceremony. Feel free to use some of them or all of them, change them and add to them. Make it your own. It's *your* Ceremony and it is paramount that it reflect what is meaningful to you.

Here are some examples:

- *Bianca planted a bush that would grow and bloom at the time of year in which she had her abortion. She felt she was giving back a life for the one she had to give up.*
- *Max and Jessica bought a mass card for their unborn child.*
- *Gina made a paper doll to represent the child she had miscarried. She kept it with her for a little while and when she was ready, she and her partner burned it and scattered the ashes in the river where they go for walks. They chose sunset to signify the closing of a time.*
- *Jack made a cradle for his unborn son and gave it to an orphanage.*

Setting.

Begin by thinking about the type of Ceremony that would be representative of your loss and be meaningful to you. Determine whether you want to do it alone or with others. Would you like to have people come together as in a traditional wake or shiva?

Gather whatever items call to you to represent your unborn child. Gather any other objects that you would like to include in the Ceremony.
Determine a time and a place.

Perform the Ceremony: I would suggest a burial or a gifting to the waters, but follow your own inner wisdom.

Allow any feelings that need to come up. You don't have to be 'nice'. Let your anger, your hurt, your sorrow, your frustrations be there. This is not the time for containment.

It is vital when you do these Ceremonies, that you make sure to do some healing Self-care afterwards.

For example:
Go for a walk.
Take a nap.
Have tea with a person dear to you.
Write in a journal, paint, or draw.
Listen or make music.
Get a massage.
Soak in a tub.

NOTES

Ceremony for a Child Given up for Adoption

- *Martha made and sent a birthday card every year to the agency that facilitated the adoption.*
- *Josie framed the copy of her sonogram showing the baby.*
- *Sam took on a foster child.*

Option 1.

Allow yourself to remember the time and circumstances that led you to giving up your child for adoption. If you have one, look at a picture of yourself at that time.

How old were you?...
What was going in your life at the time?...
What would you say to that girl or woman if you were with her today?

You might want to use the stick and ribbons techniques to wrap your thoughts, your feelings and your circumstances at the time. You might want to paint or draw a picture.
You might write a letter.

Let that part of you know that she did whatever she had to do at the time. You might do something different now, but that was then. Your decisions were informed by the circumstances of that time.

Then, take the stick or paper and bury it, burn it, or give it to the waters.

When you are done, do a Forgiveness Ceremony for yourself - (pg. 119)

Option 2.

Write a letter or make a picture for your child and bury it, burn it or gift to the waters sending the intention that s/he will receive the message in some way.

Make or buy some item that you would have liked your child to have and gift it to an orphanage.

Make sure that you do something loving and gentle for yourself after performing these Ceremonies as they can be quite emotional.

Take a warm bath...
Go for a walk...
Call a friend...
Delight in a cup of warm tea...
Play some music...

NOTES

Sudden death of a loved one

There are those times when we are suddenly faced with the death of someone close to us. This can be due to an accident, an illness, a suicide, a shooting, a war casualty, a mugging or some other sort of attack.

At the time there is often shock, bewilderment, anger, or fear as well as grief. Compounding the grief there can be a sense of guilt around having, or not having, done or said something that you believe might have prevented the death - even if that is in fact not true.

The following Ceremonies are designed to help you heal those thoughts and feelings. They can be done concurrently or consecutively. There is no right or wrong, just what seems appropriate to you under the circumstances.

The purpose of one of the Ceremonies is to bring a sense of closure to your relationship with this person to whom you did not get a chance to say good by. This is often harder if yours was a complicated relationship or if it was fraught with contention.

There may be many unsaid things, or things you wish you had not said. Actions you took, or actions you didn't take.

Make some quiet time for yourself and find a place where you can have all of your feelings and emotions without having to worry about other peoples' reactions. You may chose to do this on your own or to have a wise, caring person be there with you for support.

You may want to sit in your favorite chair, under a tree, by the water or in a place of worship. Wherever you feel safe and won't be disturbed. Turn off all of your electronics. Give yourself the time that you need to go through all of your thoughts and feelings.

You may want to write the person who died a letter, make a painting, write a song or a poem, create a sculpture, or simply speak to the air that which you could not say to that person. It doesn't have to be pretty. You may wish to tell that person how angry you are with them, how they hurt you. Or/and you might tell them how much you miss them, what they meant to you, how much you loved them. It is preferable to write in long-hand rather than on a device.

You may also use this time to ask for forgiveness for those things you did or said that may have been hurtful, and for those things you did not say or do. Take your time. It might take more than one sitting.

When you feel complete, wrap your letter or artwork with a lovely ribbon and burn it, bury it, or gift it to the waters asking that the message be conveyed, and that you may be unburdened.

Again you might chose to do this last step alone, or with people whom you know will support you in your process. This is not a panacea for your pain. It is a way to clear the energy field so that your pain is pure.

When you are done, do something loving and soothing for yourself. Whatever that means for you: a cup of tea, a walk, listening to music, dancing, shopping, or a spa treatment.

NOTES

Death of a loved one

In many cases your relationship with that person was warm, loving, and supportive. In many other cases there were bumps, and in some cases there was a lot of love, and also it was difficult and sometimes toxic or hurtful.

If it was a toxic, hurtful or abusive relationship you need to do some letting go or forgiveness first. (pg. 119)

Setting.

Here are some suggestions:

Find a place that is private and safe so you do not have to hold anything back. Allow any feelings to be present and expressed in a way that feels authentic to you. Our culture emphasizes doing our grief work in a subdued, sedate manner. Other traditions encourage crying, screaming, stomping, pulling one's hair out, tearing one's clothes and so on. Those are actually very healthy actions that help our emotions come out of our bodies rather than bottling them in.

Find a spot where you can be loud if you need/want to be and where you will not be disturbed. If you do not have access to that kind of privacy, a running shower with loud music often does the trick.

As with most all other Ceremonies you may choose to do this alone, or you might prefer to ask other people to join you, either to participate in the grief work, or to hold space for you to do your work.

Find a picture of the person that, to you, most represents who they were. If you don't have a picture or don't like any of the ones you do have, use an object that symbolizes who they were to you. It could something they gave you or that they wore, it could be a twig, a piece of jewelry, a rock, a favorite book, etc.

You might want to:
- Play one of their favorite piece of music, or one that reminds you of that person…
- Use a fragrance that they enjoyed…
- Prepare some food that they would have relished…
- Get a plant or flower…
- Write a poem, sing a song, dance, make a sculpture.

When you are finished, take some time to acknowledge the gifts that you received from that person. How did their presence enhance your life? What did you learned from them.

If you are doing this with other people, you might invite them to share how they were gifted by your loved one as well.

At end of the Ceremony, you might want to keep the things that you had gathered in a treasure box or a favorite place. You might want to burn them, to bury them or to gift them to the waters. If you had gathered a plant, you might chose to plant it in a place that they loved, or a place where you will see it often.

NOTES

Loss of a relationship

Sometimes relationships end. Perhaps a fight, perhaps a distancing, perhaps a change in living situations, perhaps just lives going in different directions.

There are many times in which the ending is smooth, subtle, almost unnoticeable, until you realize that this person is no longer part of your milieu.

However, there are times when losing a relationship, whether it is a relatively new one, or one of many years is a significant life event. It could be a life-partner, a romantic relationship, a sibling, a friend, a co-worker or anyone with whom you had a connection.

If possible, meet with the person to acknowledge the end of the relationship as it has been. Acknowledge any gifts that you received from that person and, if appropriate, the challenges that that relationship presented. If it is not possible to meet with the person, send a letter, a poem, a card or even a text. If it doesn't feel right to you to actually send the message, you can write it and shred it, bury it, burn it or whatever seems to be the appropriate venue.

What is important is that you bring closure to the relationship.
How has it benefitted you?
How has it hurt you?
What did you come to believe about yourself and others through knowing this person?

Be fully honest. At this point there is nothing to lose. However, be kind to yourself and to the other person if you share your thoughts with her/him.

Let yourself grieve in whatever way feels right to you.

Then, when you feel ready, do something loving and healing for yourself. If you can, send healing energy to the person who is no longer in your life, or with whom there is a different, less connected, relationship.

Jess was very sad when her close friend and roommate moved out saying that they were now just too different to be friends. She gave herself the time to feel lonely and to acknowledge her anger towards her friend. Then she realized that there was nothing she could do about her friend's feelings. She let herself notice her disappointment that her friend could not accept her for how she had changed. She wrote her a card acknowledging the situation, then called a new friend whom she knew accepted her as she is now.

NOTES

Loss of a job, of an opportunity, a vision, a hope, or an illusion

> 'Our real blessings often appear to us in the shape of pains, losses and disappointments; but let us have patience and we soon shall see them in their proper figures.' Joseph Addison

Often difficult events happen in our lives for which our culture typically doesn't have templates for processing or integrating. We are left wondering how to mark those events. What can we do to acknowledge them and support ourselves in moving forward?

Many of us will turn to a loved one, be it a partner, a parent, a child or a friend and tell them what happen. Nonetheless, many of us don't feel that we can do that, so we tend to keep our chin up and carry on.

If you have suffered an un-recognized loss, I recommend that you use one of the previous Ceremonies for loss and adapt it to your personal situation. It does matter—a loss is a loss.

What you experience as a loss may not be meaningful to anyone else, but it is to you. That is what matters.

When Diane did not get the job she hoped for, her aunt said: 'don't worry it's just a job, you'll get another one.' Diane was devastated that her hope for this job she had worked so hard for had been shattered. She felt doubly sad that she was not acknowledged in her disappointment and her worry about getting another job.

Sam was broken up when he was laid off from his job. He made a paper model of the office he had occupied and burned it. In doing so, he let go of his hope of becoming executive vice president at this particular firm.

Irene had hoped that the relationship with Sally would be the one. When that did not pan out she made an album of all the pictures they had taken together, wrapped it, gave thanks for all the good times, and tucked it away in the back of her closet, to maybe look at in her old age.

When her marriage broke up, Ariana gave away all her sheets, her towels and her nightgowns. It felt good to let go of those things that were so closely connected to her husband. After that, Ariana went to the store, and bought a new set of sheets, two towels and a pair of pajamas. She then took a bath (see Reclaiming your body, pg. #)

Josh's dream was to play varsity and hopefully go pro after college. In his Junior year, Josh broke his hip and couldn't keep playing. He was so upset that his life's dream was shattered that he couldn't even watch sports on TV. After some time and working with a psychotherapist and life coach, Josh burned his jersey and gave away all his sports equipment. He did keep his trophies. Josh turned his love of sports to becoming a sports manager.

NOTES

Loss of a pet

Our pets are part of our family. For some of us, they are our family. Sometimes our pets are the beings that we feel closest to, those with whom we can share our secrets.

Setting.

The death of a pet is the death of a loved one and the Ceremonies described earlier in the chapter 'loss of a loved one' would be the same with some minor adjustments.

A difficulty that periodically arises with the death of a pet is that you might have had to take her/him to the vet for a lethal injection. If that is the case, I encourage you to take some time to say good bye to your pet before you go to the vet.

If you have parts that carry some guilt about your actions, please do a Forgiveness Ceremony.

Just as in the loss of a loved one, gather items, write or draw what you would like to say and bury them, burn them or gift them to the waters.

NOTES

FORGIVENESS CEREMONIES

> Forgiveness does not change the past,
> but it does enlarge the future.
> —Paul Boese

It is important in these practices to remember that forgiveness is not pretending that something bad that was done to you, or by you, is okay or not a big deal—that would be condoning.

Forgiveness is the willingness not to hold on to the sequela of the event, which is what many Buddhist traditions call "suffering the suffering."

In forgiving someone else, you acknowledge the event or the deed and you let go of it. By that I mean, you release the beliefs and decisions that you made as a result of that event or deed. Those beliefs and decisions which continue to inform your life can prevent you from having a full, satisfying life. For example, deciding never to trust anyone because someone betrayed you.

In forgiving yourself, you take responsibility for your actions, and if possible, make amends to the person you feel you've wronged. If that is not possible, write a letter, draw a picture, compose a poem, or write song to that person and bury it, burn it, or gift to the waters.

In forgiving another person, you can talk to them about the hurt that they caused you. Hopefully, they will acknowledge their wrong-doing—whether it was intentional or not—and you can gradually mend the relationship over time. If, for whatever reason, it is not possible to connect with that person, write a letter, draw a picture, compose a poem, write a song and bury it, burn it, or gift it to the waters letting go of the weight that you have carried in hurt or resentment.

I like to take a large rock and place it on my chest. Allowing for all the pain, the hurt, the resentment, the anger, the sorrow, etc., to be conveyed to the rock. I then bury it, saying that I no longer wish to carry this weight.

It is also important to not be overly judgmental either of yourself, or of the other person, and to develop compassion for the difficulties that brought that person, or yourself, to do this wrong action.

NOTES

Forgiving yourself

It is particularly important in this Ceremony to be very gentle with and towards yourself and to create a setting that is warm, supportive and loving. For some of you being outdoors creates a sense of safety, privacy and spaciousness. For others, going to a house of worship creates the proper environment. For some others a special spot where you live or any place where you feel welcomed and safe.

Setting.

As in the setting for the meditations, begin by grounding yourself with a few slow deep breaths. Gently bring your attention into your heart ushering in the finest, gentlest energy you can imagine.

You might imagine a ray of sun light, or moon light, the gaze of someone who you know loves and accepts you as you are, the energy of a higher being, or any image or feeling that will bring warmth into your heart area.

Now, with great compassion allow any parts that hold guilt to gently show themselves to you. They may be recent events, or actions from long ago.

Ask those parts not to overwhelm you. If there are several parts or situations, ask that they take turns and show themselves one by one.

Connect with the part(s) that holds the guilt, or shame, until you can feel caring, compassion and understanding towards it. Maybe that part's actions were indeed noxious and possibly harmful either towards yourself or towards others.

Ask that part how it came to be and what led it to behave in the way that it did.

As the part shows/tells you what and why, what happened, happened, let yourself understand and recognize that how that part behaved was the best s/he could have done at the time under the circumstances both inner and outer. Possibly it wasn't the best, notwithstanding it was the option that seemed available at the time.

Gently ask the part to release the energy of guilt or shame that it has been carrying.

You can do that by using the stick technique (pg. 64), placing the guilt or shame on a water vessel, (pg. 81) placing it in a balloon, (pg. 65) or using any of the techniques outlined earlier. You can also create your own way of releasing this negative energy.

Another possibility, is to imagine this energy as a color, a shape, a sensation, or an image. Then imagine sending this energy out of your physical, emotional and mental bodies. You can send it out to the universe, to the sun, to the moon, to the earth, to the waters or to any other place that seems suitable.

After releasing this negative, shameful, guilty energy, bring back into yourself any wisdom or teaching that you received from this experience. You might receive it as a message, or an idea, or a felt sense. Ask your parts that you might handle the next situation with greater compassion and wisdom towards all parties involved.

When you are done, bring back into yourself loving kindness and compassion

Julie grew up in a violent household. She learned to use belligerent behavior to deal with situations. Now an adult, having moved away from those circumstances, she felt guilty about some of her own behavior. She chose to let go of her guilt by making paper dolls of all the parts that she identified as having behaved in violent ways and burning them one at a time, honoring why and how they had behaved and requesting that from here forth she find greater gentleness in her interactions with herself and others.

NOTES

Forgiving others

Whoever hurt you or abused you, physically, emotionally or in any other way is responsible for her/his actions. They need to deal with the consequences of those actions within themselves.

That is their business, not yours.

The pain, the hurt, the sense of betrayal, the beliefs and decisions that you made about yourself and your life as a result of those events are real. However, holding on to anger, to resentment or to vengeance toward that other person continues to hurt you and narrows your capacity for a fulfilled, happy life.

Forgiveness Ceremonies are very similar to Letting Go Ceremonies, because you are, in effect, letting go of the connection to the person(s) who hurt you. You are also releasing the beliefs and decisions that you made about yourself and the world as a consequence of those events.

Claude AnShin Thomas, a Vietnam veteran who became a Zen Buddhist monk says that how we feel and think is a direct consequence of what happened to us. However, we do not have to continue to be informed by those beliefs and decisions. We can chose (easier said than done - but totally feasible) to live our life free of those resentments, those fears, those beliefs and those decisions.

Here are Ceremonies I particularly like, although you can use any of the Letting Go Ceremonies that resonate with you and tweak them to fit your particular needs and desires.

Setting.

Throwing rocks into water (Similar to Casting Away Ceremony, (pg. 79).

I prefer the ocean because I like the sound of the surf crashing, and the power of the waves, but any body of water that is outside is fine.

I like rocks, but you can use any object that seems appropriate: seeds, leaves, bread crumbs, pieces of wood, some writing, something that belonged to the person who hurt you, and so forth. I recommend that you use something that is biodegradable, but whatever works for you is suitable.

One of my clients threw her ex-boyfriend's very expensive earphones in a lake, as a symbol of how she felt he was overly self-involved and that he never listened to her.

As you toss the item(s) into the waters say—out loud if you can—what you are casting off.

Let yourself feel whatever feelings come up. Crying, shaking, yelling are all good ways to release emotions.

- I am casting off the belief that I am dirty because you hurt me ...
- I am casting off my shame...
- I am casting off my pent up anger towards you...
- I am casting off all the negative comments you made about me...
- I am casting off my desire to hurt you back...
- I am casting off ...

When you feel done, take some of the water and wash away from your physical, mental and emotional bodies any remaining connection with those who hurt you.

I like to say:
I am cleaned of any negativity.
I am free of all those beliefs.
I am open to the truth of who I am.

And if you can:
I set you free to be healed.

When you are finished, do something loving and nurturing for yourself.
Get a cup of tea or coffee and enjoy its warmth and flavor,
sit and enjoy the fresh air,
go home and cuddle up with a good book,
write in your journal,
connect with a loved one,
make a painting, write a song, sing ...

NOTES

Using sticks, yarn ribbons, etc.

Setting.

As in the Generic Letting Go Ceremony, (pg.69) you can wrap a stick with a variety of ribbons, yarn or other materials, insert words, pictures or symbols.

Another way is to make a knot in a strand of yarn, of ribbon, etc., for each person, each instance, or group of situations in which you were hurt.

Each time you make a knot you name it

- This is for all the times you yelled at me.
- This is for the times you shamed me and belittled me.
- This is for the time I couldn't go to the prom because you tore my dress.
- This is for the times you ignored me.
- This is for the time I had to stay home because I was black and blue from your blows.
- This is for the times I had to take care of the little kids because you were passed out drunk.

Take your time ... let yourself cry, shout, feel the hurt, be angry, allowing those held in emotions to come out of your system.

When you feel done, bury, burn or gift the stick or knots to the waters. Ask that all that has been put into those knots be transmuted and that you may be free to be who you are.

It is important to complete the Ceremony by doing something restorative and nurturing for yourself.

NOTES

Writing, drawing or making a collage

Setting.

As you do this exercise, allow yourself to have any feelings or thoughts that come up. Be gentle with yourself and hold those thoughts and feelings with compassion.

Find a piece of paper - any kind that you like. You can use plain paper, construction paper, card stock, cardboard, or lettuce leaves! Pick out materials that appeal to you.

You might want to use one piece of paper for each instance, or person you are wishing to release, or use one to represent all the instances in which you felt hurt or abused.

Write, draw, color, or make a collage of the ways that you were hurt. Take your time. Let any emotions or thoughts be present. This is not the time to either contain or repress.

Write, draw, color, or make a collage of the ways you are still holing on to the hurts that were perpetrated upon you. Take your time

Write, draw, color, or make a collage of the ways in which your life was impacted, and the beliefs and decisions that you made as result of those events. Take your time.

When you are done, take your writings or drawings and burn them, bury, them, shred them or gift them to the waters

Ask that you may be released from any connection to those events and be free to be the beautiful, powerful, amazing, being that you are.

NOTES

A stretch—after forgiveness

Once you feel complete with your Forgiveness Ceremony, you might choose to take an extra step. Endeavor to understand the circumstances, or life situations, that made the person(s) who hurt you behave in such a deplorable way towards you.

Setting.

If you can, send compassion for their suffering, and ask that they too be healed and made whole. You might also use one of the preceding Ceremonies, and tweak it to apply to the other person.

For example, you might find an item that is representative of the person who hurt you, or an object that is illustrative of the harm they did to you. Bury that item, or burn it, or gift it to the waters, asking that the person who hurt you be cleared of their demons. Request that they too, might be set free to live a life that is good and healthy.

There is a Buddhist mantra that I have found brings me solace and allows me to forgive those towards whom I hold resentments.

May I be free from suffering,
and the roots of suffering.
May all sentient beings be from suffering,
and the roots of suffering.
May I be at peace,
and find the roots of peace.
May all beings be at peace and find the roots of peace.
May I be happy,
and find the roots of happiness.
May all beings be happy,
and find the roots of happiness.

And again remember that forgiveness is not condoning. It is freeing yourself from the albatross of holding on to negative feelings and beliefs.

Mike made matchstick figures of the people who had hurt him as a child. He then burned each one separately saying: I set me free, I set you free. He then went to a sauna to clear every cell of his body from any leftover energy.

Alexa danced her liberation from being held forcefully and raped. She gave her body the permission to move that had been taken away from her, and imagined her rapist dancing away, also free to move in a good healthy way and re-owning his body.

Bill and Camille wrote down all the ways that they blamed the other for the dysfunction of their relationship. Together, they went to bury their writings, then planted a fruit tree to symbolize cooperation and fruitfulness in each of their lives.

NOTES

CELEBRATIONS

The more you praise and celebrate your life,
the more there is in life to celebrate.
—Oprah Winfrey

> Joy shared is double joy, Sorrow shared is half sorrow.
> —Swedish saying

This quote has become one of my favorites as I believe it touches into the truth of our humanity.

Our western culture celebrations are often based on political events: presidents' day, labor day, armistice day, religious events: Christmas, Hanukkah, Ramadan, Easter, Passover, New Year, or on acknowledging groups: Mothers Day, Fathers Day, Teachers Day, etc. They are not personal. More personal celebrations such as birthdays, weddings, births, and graduations are also based on a cultural template that may or may not fit into your personal ideas or mythology.

Most importantly in my view, we do not have any templates to celebrate achievements, insights, changes of job or world view, a coming of age (whether you are 8, 13, 48, 64) or of any events that are not socially recognized as meriting a celebration.

A long time ago I read Mutant Message Down Under by Marlo Morgan. Some people claimed that she had made it up. Maybe. Regardless, I thought the message was powerful. One of the things that struck me in that story is that to me, it is the story of a tribe where people follow their heart and are acknowledged for what/who they are or who they want to be at various times of their life. One of the passages that struck me was when a member of the tribe who had done a certain job for years and done it well, gathered the tribe and announced that from now on he was going to do something else and would therefore be an apprentice. A few months later, that person gathered the tribe again and announced that he was now proficient in his new metier and was acknowledge as that. Another while later, he again gathered the tribe and announced he was now a master at that trade and was recognized as such by the tribe.

Of course we can poke lots of holes in that tale. What was kindled in me was the freedom and the societal acknowledgment that we can become truer to who we are as time goes by. We do not have much of that kind of acknowledgements in our culture, unless the move is spectacular, like giving up being a janitor to become a star singer, or getting a very big promotion at work.

For many (not all) people even our rites of passage feel flat and not overly personally meaningful.

Examples of unrecognized events would be: developing a new attitude or mind set about the way we choose to live our lives or the way we choose to relate to certain people or events; having the courage to do or say something that might have been frightening; choosing a non-traditional career or choosing not to go for the promotion because of the way it would impact the rest of our lives; arriving at a new experience of ourselves and of who we are in the world, etc.

The following Ceremonies are suggestions of ways to celebrate, acknowledge, rejoice, accept and deepen our experiences. Like all other Ceremonies in this book, you may choose to do it on your own or to share it with some important people in your life. I recommend the latter because I believe that we are not witnessed sufficiently in our growth and change.

In my role as therapist, one of my favorite Ceremony of acknowledgment is one that happens in the moment to recognize a change. We take a stone, a shell, a bead or a very small object and we imbue it with the new insight, point of view, attitude, or belief that was just arrived at through our work. I then suggest to my client that she carry that object in her pocket as a reminder, reinforcement and anchor for the new belief, insight, decision, etc. Obviously, you can do this on your own. I still have in my pocket a stone my own therapist gave me 20 years ago. It connects me to her and to the work that we did together that has helped me become more and more who I have wanted to be.

You might chose to write a letter, a poem, a musical piece, create performance, go for a walk and declare your new found wisdom to the beings of nature.

You might set up a special moment: a candle, a quiet cup of tea to share with a loved one and take in their enjoyment of your moment. Let them treat you in some way to acknowledge the moment.

Get flowers or a small object to remind you of your beauty and place them someplace where you will see them often, take a bubble bath, go shopping, or all of the above ... use your imagination.

Another favorite

Setting.

Create a treasure box. You can buy an attractive box or use one that you already have and if need be decorate it. In it place any accolade or recognition that you received. When someone gives you a compliment, write it down and put it in the box, when someone sends you a note or a card, put it in the box. Look at it often and relish the feeling of acknowledgment again.

When you want to celebrate a part of you that has grown or changed, become freer, happier, stronger etc. find a way to concretize it and put it in the box. Look at those items often, particularly when you feel yourself slipping into negative thoughts or beliefs.

You can also use any of the Ceremony suggested in Creating Ceremonies (pg. 63) and focus it with positive intentions such as in the Bringing In ceremonies.

Caleb celebrated having conquered his fear of the dark by removing his night lights and replacing them with star shine in the dark decals.

Isabel celebrated feeling better about her body by taking a rose water bath.

Sylvia celebrated her new attitude towards people by taking pictures of everyone she loved and creating a slide show. Then she invited them to come watch it.

Mario planted a small evergreen tree to celebrate that he could be a strong man as well as gentle enough to sway in the wind.

Inez bought a dozen multi-colored flowers and gifted them to the waters to carry her sense of freedom and her ability to flow.

NOTES

Dear Reader,

I hope you've found this little book helpful. It has been my pleasure to share these meditations and ceremonies with you.

Shungo—a Quechua word that means from my heart to yours.

I can be contacted at <u>moniquelanglcsw.com</u>

Made in the USA
Las Vegas, NV
22 October 2021